GROWING UP CLINTON

Growing Up Clinton

The Lives,
Times and
Tragedies of
America's
Presidential
Family

Roger Clinton

with Jim Moore

THE SUMMIT PUBLISHING GROUP

THE SUMMIT PUBLISHING GROUP
One Arlington Centre, 1112 East Copeland Road, Fifth Floor
Arlington, Texas 76011

Copyright © 1995 by Roger C. Clinton. All rights reserved. No part of this book may be reproduced or transmitted in any form or by any means, electronic or mechanical, including photocopying, recording, or by any information storage and retrieval system, without the written permission of the publisher, except where permitted by law.

Printed in the United States of America.

99 98 97 95 1 2 3 4 5

ISBN: 1-56530-178-1

Book design by David Sims

Other Summit Publishing Books by Jim Moore include:
Conspiracy of One: The Definitive Book on the Kennedy Assassination
Clinton: Young Man in a Hurry
Rampage: America's Largest Family Mass Murder

For Our Mothers;

And for Tyler Cassidy Clinton,

who has brought the music full circle.

TABLE OF CONTENTS

✻

PREFACE

I guess you could say that I've learned my lesson the hard way: Setting someone's life to words is a monumental struggle.

When that someone is the brother of the president of the United States, it compounds the effort required.

And when that someone is Roger Cassidy Clinton, the job is darned near impossible.

I've known Roger since I was a teenager. We count each other as good friends. The reason we were able to write this book, I believe, is because we have almost nothing in common.

Roger and I are nothing alike in temperament and lifestyle. His experiences in the fast-paced world of Hollywood fascinate me; I rather suspect that he sometimes yearns for the peace and quiet I've enjoyed for so many years in Arkansas and Texas. When Roger feels strongly about something, he's incredibly hard to reason with. I sit back and try to think of ways to change what I don't like.

Roger likes to sleep in; I'm up early. Roger stays up late; if I make it through the 10:00 P.M. news, I'm lucky. Roger loves sports; I seldom know who's playing. Roger loves to be in the middle of crowds of people; I'd rather be at home alone with Kathy. Roger lives for the moment; I plan everything.

Our only common ground is that we both grew up in Arkansas. Our differences continued to fascinate me long past the point when other writers would have given up. This book exists because we are so dissimilar.

All told, we spent nearly two years on this project. I did it for a reason: I think Roger has a unique story to tell. His life and his struggles captivated me; I hope I've done them justice here.

Roger Cassidy Clinton is three things: unique, talented, and inspiring. I've never met anyone quite like him. I have been surprised by the depth of his musical abilities. And, his story can inspire all of us to overcome the hardship and adversity in our own lives.

Like his brother, Roger goes to work when the deck is stacked against him. He has the ability to foresee circumstances and situations before they occur and develop the mindset necessary to take advantage of them. The only other common bond Rog and I share is tenacity; neither of us knows the meaning of the work "quit."

Even if Roger and I are so dissimilar, I can still admire him. I've argued with him, been frustrated, hurt, and angry, and I still come away liking the guy. Perhaps the people who dislike Roger lack my patience. Or, maybe they don't look deep enough to see what really makes the man tick. This book should answer that question for them.

I hope that Roger and I will be friends for years to come. I'm glad that I could help tell his story.

Here's to you, pal.

— Jim Moore

✳

ACKNOWLEDGMENTS

Our heartfelt appreciation to: Mike Towle, Len Oszustowicz, Vicki Crawford, Nancy Crawford Adkins, Mark Hulme, Molly Clinton, and Kathy Moore.

Our special thanks to: Lynda Dixon, Emilie Martin, Carolyn Huber, Bill and Hillary Rodham Clinton, and Nancy Morton.

And, our thanks to: Edith Irons, Ronnie and Charlie Marstaller, Lori Shelton, Jim Pinkston, Loretta at BSC, Walter Kaudelka, John Robison, Ross Barnes, Beth Jones, Gorma Muratore, Tom Rettig, Melinda Gassaway, David Vann, Marge Mitchell, Mike and Dixie Seba, Mike Pakkis, Virginia Kelley's Birthday Club, and Bear.

CHAPTER ONE

GROWING UP CLINTON

I was home from school with a nasty headache, resting in bed. My room was at the end of a long hallway that ran from the living room across the length of the house. I could hear my parents arguing again, although I couldn't make out what they were saying. Suddenly, there was a strange noise—a sort of soft thud. I got out of bed in my underwear, ran about fifteen feet down the hallway, and peered into the kitchen. From there, I could see into the small utility room.

My father was bending my mother backwards over the washing machine, grasping her throat in one hand and a pair of scissors in the other.

Shocked by what I was seeing, I stood helpless and frozen, unable even to scream. Finally, I pulled myself away and ran out the front door to the house next door, where my brother was studying with the Millers' son. I burst into the Miller house without knocking. "Bubba, come quick!" I screamed. "Daddy's killing Dado!"

We ran back to the house, rushing through the open garage door. My brother opened the door that led into the utility room and the kitchen, wrenched my mother from my father's grasp, and shoved her back next to me. My father stood there, his eyes raging, the scissors still clutched in his hand.

"You will never hurt either of them again," Bill shouted at my father. "If you want them, you'll have to go through me." Daddy dropped the scissors and began to take off his belt as if to beat him. Bill pulled us along with him into the living room, shutting the door in Daddy's face.

Mother and I were both crying as Bill sat us down on the couch and knelt to comfort us. After a moment he stood up and turned to deal with Daddy in the kitchen. Within seconds we could hear them shouting, but Daddy was no match for Bill anymore. This time, Daddy left the house.

Bill was sixteen then, still a kid to many, but he was much more than that to Mother and me.

That vivid memory of my childhood epitomized life in a "dysfunctional" family. I qualify that term because it has become so overused as to be almost meaningless and also because all families have difficulties, although some more severe than others. However, I feel that the abuse inflicted upon us by my father forced our family to reconfigure itself in ways that were not really "normal," although they were necessary.

I was only six years old when the incident described above occurred, and from that moment on I lived in fear of my father, constantly hoping that something would happen to rescue our family from him. During the 1992 presidential campaign, one of our neighbors on Scully Street in Hot Springs told a reporter, "I didn't know Roger (Sr.) was *that* bad." To a small child, he was terrifying.

I always thought of my dad as a cruel, mean, frightening man. Growing up, I never thought he really cared about my mother, my brother, or me. By the time I was old enough to understand what was happening, my parents' affection for each other was nearly extinguished. Mother tried to protect and shield me from my father—from their arguments and fighting. Unfortunately, Daddy was drunk about ninety percent of the time, so I rarely saw any other side of him. Every time we heard the front door open, we would pray it wasn't him.

The good times during those early years were few and far between. Even today, I can't forget the nights when pain and fright gripped me. Lying awake late at night now, with my wife Molly asleep beside me, I think of my son Tyler and am glad he won't have to endure what I did.

Because my relationship with my father was tainted with fear, I tried to spend as much time as possible with my mother. My earliest memory is sitting at my mother's makeup bench with her while she got ready for work. She went to the hospital an hour or so before my dad left for work and my brother went to school. Mother's job as a nurse-anesthetist took her away from home a great deal, so I was up early with her almost every morning.

I don't recall much about my abusive father before I was five years old. Bill was really more of an important figure to me. He was almost obsessive about wanting me near him and was my best friend, my guardian, my father, and my role model.

➻ EARLY ON ➺

I think I loved kindergarten because it took me away from my father. I attended Miss Cooper's Kinder-Coop, in Hot Springs. Miss Cooper was licensed to run a kindergarten in her home, and she had arts and crafts for us, along with toys and swing sets.

Most mornings, my father would take me to the Clinton auto dealership where he worked, then I would ride to kindergarten with a kindly black man named Early. My father's brothers owned the dealership, and Daddy worked in the parts department. Sometimes on Saturdays he'd take me down to the dealership and I'd sit on the parts counter while he handled the customers.

I looked forward to getting home every day even though kindergarten—and later, grade school—became an oasis of sorts for me. Mother was usually home when I got there although she put in long hours at the hospital. She was a very disciplined person and worked hard to provide for us. Being away from her was tough; being at school with my friends made it bearable.

While Mother was working, and before I started grade school, she hired a wonderful lady named Earlene White to take care of me and keep house. Mother couldn't afford to pay her very much, and Earlene loved my family, so she worked for practically nothing. I'll always be grateful for her care and affection while I was growing up. After I started school, Earlene would get me up each morning, make sure I was dressed properly and had eaten my breakfast, then see me off for the day.

One of Earlene's sons, incidentally, is James "Duck" White, who was one of the "Purple People Eaters" of the Minnesota Vikings. When I entered my freshman year in high school, "Duck" took it upon himself to watch over me, just as his mother had done when I was younger.

Another housekeeper during my earliest years was Miss Walters. I always called her "Waffers." With these two ladies, along with Mother, I didn't want for love and attention. Earlene White and "Waffers" really raised me. Mother worked all day, and she trusted them to take care of me while she was at the hospital.

All the time, I kept wishing the situation with my father would improve. It never did. Until I was about six, we were living in a house on Park Avenue, in the older part of Hot Springs. Many evenings my mother would sneak Bill and me out of the house and take us to the nearby Capri Motel, owned by our friends Annie and Charlie Tyler. Escaping from home was the only way to avoid my father's drunken rages, although at the time I couldn't understand why we couldn't stay at home and live a normal life like the other kids I knew.

While I was finishing kindergarten, my parents divorced, only to remarry again some months later. Between the divorce and remarriage, Mother, Bill, and I moved to the outskirts of Hot Springs. Mother purchased a home on Scully Street so I could attend Oaklawn Elementary School. I think she liked being close to the Oaklawn racetrack, too.

➼ SCULLY STREET ☞

The house at 213 Scully was a modern, early sixties' style suburban home with a large backyard. Bill often organized football
games in the backyard, designating two large pine trees as goal-
posts and the swing set as the out-of-bounds marker. He and his
friends—guys like Guido Hassen, Jim Case, Ronnie Cecil, David
Dunham, and David Leopoulos—would choose up sides, and I'd
be the center.

In Arkansas, children play football year-round. Even snow
and ice don't delay the neighborhood scrimmages. Sometimes,
though, when snow was on the ground, Bill would put me on my
sled and pull me over the ice. I loved it, and he didn't seem to
mind the cold as long as I was content.

I also had a little red wagon I dragged around the house and
up and down the street. In my room were two large stuffed teddy
bears and a menagerie of other stuffed animals. My fondness for
stuffed animals continues—I have a giant stuffed bear in my
home today. My son Tyler will love it when he gets a little older.

Mother bought me a parakeet named "Sport." How could
you *not* get along with an animal named Sport? One day, Sport
didn't want to play with me, and when I tried to prod him into
action I accidentally broke his neck. I learned a powerful lesson
about persistence that day. More appropriately, I learned how to
temper my stick-to-itiveness and to make sure my intent is good
and genuine. I get my persistence from Mother, I think. Bill has
it, too.

The year we moved to Scully Street I started first grade. School was a wonderful place, except for one thing. I heard all the other kids talking about the camping and fishing trips they'd taken with their dads, and I didn't really have a dad to talk about. Instead, I told them about my mother and brother.

Christmas that year was just like every other Christmas when I was a kid—spectacular. That was the year I got a really good bicycle. I didn't get lots of other presents—we couldn't afford much—but mother always went out of her way to make the Yuletide an enjoyable experience for all of us. I would help her and Bill decorate the tree, hanging the ornaments and icicles. On Christmas morning there would be presents from Santa to unwrap. There was the bicycle, of course; another Christmas, the one after my father died, I received a basketball goal. I don't know how Mother found the time, but she created some great Christmas memories for my brother and me.

Other memories and traditions lived in the minds of extended family members, and they passed them on to Bill and me. Sometimes, on the weekends, my father would take us up through the winding streets of Hot Springs to see his parents—my grandparents. Bill and I would sit on their front porch and listen to the wit and wisdom of Poppy Al or pay rapt attention to Momma Clinton as she talked about the covered wagon days. As a young girl, she'd crossed the country in a pioneer caravan, and the stories she told were spellbinding. She spent a great deal of time cultivating an enormous garden and canning everything. Often, when we came to visit, she made me my favorite dessert—banana pudding.

I could have stayed with Momma Clinton and Poppy Al forever, but there was never enough time. My brother, especially, was becoming a busy young man. He was involved in all sorts of extracurricular activities at school, and beginning to develop a social life as well. When Bill started dating, he'd often take me with him. This was never as awkward as it sounds. He'd tell the young woman I was going along, and that was it. I always enjoyed cruising around Hot Springs with my brother and his friends. I remember I liked most of my brother's girlfriends, and several—like Mauria Jackson and Mary Jo Nelson—remain good family friends.

Bill loved driving my father's bright yellow Kaiser "Henry J." convertible, the car I tried to recreate on the cover of my first album, "Nothing Good Comes Easy." Bill would drive me around town in the Henry J., and we'd sing the latest songs—like the new Seekers hit, "We'll Build A World of Our Own." Other favorites were "I Know I'll Never Find Another You" and Elvis's "Hound Dog." My brother had a terrific voice, and I was impressed with his singing. During the presidential campaign, of course, much was made of Bill's imitations of Elvis Presley.

By the time I entered second grade, my father was spending less and less time at home. Mother, Bill, and I were relieved that most of the confrontations had finally ended. As I grew older, I wondered from time to time what my mother had seen in him. "He was a wonderful man," she'd tell me, trying to explain the love she felt for him. "He loves you boys," Mother would say, "He's not a bad man, he's a sick man." Despite her assurances, I lived in fear of him; and if he ever loved me, I wasn't aware of it.

Of course, I now know that alcoholism is a disease, a sickness which afflicts all kinds of people. Perhaps, if I had been able to think of Daddy as suffering from a disease, I would have been better able to relate to him as a child, although I kind of doubt it. For all children of alcoholics, there are no second chances at childhood. My opportunity to raise Tyler in a different way is as close to a second chance as I'll ever get.

Nevertheless, I was able to leave family problems behind for hours at a time, especially with playmates like Vicki Crawford and Teresa and Alberta Hassen. We'd play after school and during the summer months. Soon, I entered the second grade in Mrs. Warner's class, and I like to think I was a pretty normal kid, shooting paper-wads and trying not to get cooties from the girls.

Around this time my father's health began to deteriorate and Bill, a high school senior, was preparing to move halfway across the country to attend Georgetown University. When he left home, I was devastated, even though he would come back to Arkansas fairly often during those four years in college, and Mother and I went to Georgetown a couple of times as well.

Bill and I corresponded frequently. I wrote to him about music—I was listening to a lot of Elvis and Beatles—and thoroughbred horse racing, passions we all shared. Mother took me to the Oaklawn racetrack, before I could even walk. We'd sit in an area called "Tri-Vesta" on the back side of the racetrack, watching horses run by for hours. She even taught me how to read using the racing form.

When Bill wrote back, he always told me to take care of Mother and myself, and to study hard. He urged me to practice the saxophone, but that didn't take. The extent of my repertoire is probably a few measures of "Pink Panther" and "Twinkle, Twinkle, Little Star."

The times when Bill came home were very happy events for me. I remember hand-printing banners that read "Welcome Home, Bubba" and hanging them in the living room and outside the house. When he came home, it was as if he'd never left.

As he went through college, I worked my way through grade school. Mrs. House was my third grade teacher, and I had Miss Scruggs in fourth grade, probably the toughest teacher I had. I really loved Mrs. Munk, my fifth grade teacher. Miss Whittington guided me through sixth grade and helped me make the difficult transition to junior high. I remember getting into mischief—once, I carved my name on my desk in Miss Whittington's room. Miss Whittington still lives in Hot Springs, and whenever I see her, I can count on being reminded about that misdemeanor.

My teachers and my mother did their best to discipline me; they did what was necessary, even if that included the occasional spanking. Back then, of course, no one cried "child abuse" if their child was spanked in school. I was spanked at home and at school if I misbehaved, and most of the time I deserved it. Regardless of the spankings, the authority figures in my life, excepting my dad, went out of their way to show me they loved and cared about me, reinforcement I desperately needed since my dad finally passed away when I was eleven years old.

It might sound cruel, but I thought he'd never die. Daddy had developed terminal cancer, and he came home to Arkansas for the last time after spending six weeks at Duke University Hospital, in Durham, North Carolina. Again and again over a two-week period, I heard people tell me, "This is your dad's last day." When he finally died, I felt mainly relief. But I was also angry—angry at God for leaving me without a father. I couldn't understand why my family had to suffer; why my dad had to be mean and sick—and now dead. My confused child's tortured logic brought no answers to these questions.

Daddy's death was not the only significant event occurring around that time. Bill's four years at Georgetown were drawing to a close and Mother and I went there to see him graduate in that spring of 1968. I was awfully proud of him when he was selected as a Rhodes scholar and went to study at Oxford in the fall of 1968. Except for a single trip he made to Arkansas, I didn't see him for the next two years.

As he left for England, I went into the seventh grade; and at junior high, I felt my brother's absence a little less keenly. I had new friends and new things to do.

A GENTLEMAN'S GENTLEMAN

When I was in the seventh grade, my mother remarried. Her new husband was a wonderful man named Jeff Dwire; a gentleman's gentleman. In a world of people who are lucky to do just one thing well, he had accomplished much: He was an award-winning hairdresser and the owner of "Jeff's Hair Fashions," a ten-operator beauty salon in Hot Springs. He also built homes, mostly for the Tandy Homes company in Lewisville, Arkansas, about a hundred miles southwest of Hot Springs.

I don't remember a lot about their courtship. They would go out on the lake, or to the racetrack. At first, when he did come to the house, it was uncomfortable for me. I wanted Mother to be happy—there were signs of that—and I needed a father figure. On the other hand, at twelve, the "bad stuff" in a marriage still scared me. So she sat us down in the living room and swore she wouldn't move ahead without our okay. After some hesitation on my part, Big Brother and I gave them our blessing.

Mother and I were still living in the house on Scully Street, and Jeff moved in with us after the wedding. He was a very sincere and honest man, making it quite clear to me that he wasn't trying to take my dad's place. Instead, he genuinely wanted to take care of Mother and be a part of our family. All the pain, violence, and fear Mother and I shared ended when Daddy died; but since my father had been the cause of all the grief, I viewed Jeff with great trepidation. He understood and made allowances for my feelings, often going out of his way to make me feel secure.

I quickly grew to love Jeff. He took me everywhere—to shoot pool, fishing, bowling. I have a special fondness for pinball machines and malteds that is associated with him. He taught me the elegant art of shooting pool, and I discovered that my skill with a pool cue allowed me to generate something of an income. I had other odd jobs, but as I grew older I managed to make most of my spending money by shooting pool. Jeff might not have been pleased that I'd turned his gentleman's game into something more plebeian, but I made some change and enjoyed a certain envied status among my friends.

I would play with friends and strangers, usually at the bowling alley. We'd bet anywhere from five to twenty dollars per game, sometimes more, but we never got much above a fifty- or sixty-dollar wager. I wouldn't call myself a pool hustler: I just played with my friends and won money doing it. Of course, I lost some money, too.

Jeff worked hard—not too hard, but hard enough—to show Mother and me he really loved us, building an extra room for me at the back of the house. We called it "Roger's Roost" and there was a pool table, a long storage chest with a cushion on top for seating, and a sliding glass door that led to the backyard. I decorated the walls with blacklight paint and blacklight posters of some of my favorite rock groups—REO Speedwagon, Grand Funk Railroad—and I had a large Alice Cooper poster on my bedroom door. I had been collecting ball caps for some time, and there was plenty of room to store my collection. Some of my caps are with me in California now, while others—a few that I've had since junior high—are still at Mother's lake house.

My bedroom door, Jeff decided, should be preserved for posterity. It's a real work of art, covered with little stickers, paint, and a dozen other media. That door is still at my mother's house on Lake Hamilton. I wonder what Tyler will make of it when he's old enough to appreciate it.

Mother and Jeff had been married more than a year when Bill came back to the United States from England. He left again a month or so later and headed back to the East Coast for three years at Yale University to study law. Unlike the two years he'd spent in Oxford, Bill was able to drive home fairly often during his tenure at Yale.

When Bill left for Yale, I was fourteen years old. Over time, Jeff Dwire became the male role model in my life, and I developed a deep and abiding affection for him. I don't think my brother bonded as much with Jeff, as he wasn't looking for a father figure at that point in his life—certainly not the way I was. Jeff was everything my real father hadn't been—loving, concerned about my mother, considerate and helpful. He gave us a sense of stability that had been completely lacking when my dad was alive.

Jeff would always tell me my brother would be a major player in American politics, but that I would make the "big money." Come to think of it, though, he never told me what I'd be doing to make the big bucks. He tried to prepare me for the success he envisioned by teaching me to be a well-mannered gentleman. If he left me with nothing else, Jeff often repeated, he'd leave me with manners. At mealtime, he was a friendly but strict disciplinarian. My hands were where they were supposed to be, in my lap with no leaning on the table. To this day, I have excellent table manners.

In the midst of this pleasant time, Jeff became ill but didn't want to slow down.

"I have no intention," he would tell Bill and me, "of letting your mother bring home the bacon." Aware that continued exertion could eventually kill him, Jeff slowed down, but he wasn't going to quit.

For him, compromise meant less time at the beauty salon, and his after-work routine became less rigorous. Before, he would come home at the end of the day and head for his woodworking tools and shop equipment in the garage. He built birdhouses, doghouses, and mailboxes—all with a craftsman's touch. Now, Jeff came home and went to bed instead.

I wanted to please and emulate Jeff, so I decided to go to work during the summer to prove to us both that I could work hard. One of my jobs was lifeguarding at the Velda Rose Hotel in Hot Springs. Many of the hotel guests were prospective buyers from out of state, looking for timeshares in Hot Springs Village. One such family was the Sheltons, down from Joplin, Missouri. I first saw Lori and her family when they came to the pool to swim. Lori was fourteen then, with a beautiful smile and an infectious laugh.

Lori and I started writing letters back and forth after she and her family returned to Joplin. Since I loved to write, corresponding with Lori was a real pleasure, and I learned more and more about her through the letters she wrote me.

Lori became one of the best friends I've ever had, and our friendship has endured for two decades now. Like most kids growing up, we fell in love a little but grew out of it with the years.

That same summer, Bill came back home to Arkansas. He'd received his law degree from Yale and had accepted a job teaching law at the University of Arkansas at Fayetteville, way up in the northwest corner of the state. I was sixteen and had my own life, but being able to see him on weekends was a real treat.

In the summer of 1973, I turned seventeen. This was a difficult time, as Jeff was in great pain most of the time. "I'm going to go out the same way I came in," he said. In any beauty salon, especially one with ten beauty operators, there's always a lot of hairspray. Over the years, Jeff had ingested massive quantities of hairspray. I think the stuff slowly poisoned him: it certainly affected his breathing. He also suffered from diabetes. With a hole in one of his heart valves, Jeff was a very sick man. Even so, the full extent of his condition didn't manifest itself until late 1973.

It tore my heart out to watch Jeff suffer. He was in such excruciating pain, it became difficult for him to lie down or sleep, and he began spending his nights in another bedroom so Mother could sleep undisturbed. Quite often during the night, Jeff would get up, kneel beside the bed, and wait for the pain to subside. Often, he would actually cry because the pain was so bad.

His doctors advised him to change his lifestyle, to cut back on his activity and become more sedentary. If he gave up the beauty salon, started walking every day, and spent his time around the house, he might live another ten or twenty years. Jeff refused to stop working, even though he said he loved us desperately.

"You all might as well get used to me not being around in another year," he told us. It became obvious he wanted to die working, and as it turned out, he got his wish.

I listened to Jeff crying in pain and agony, and I would go into my bedroom, shut the door, and cry to God. Why? Why was He letting this happen? Why was He torturing us all over again? Why was He hurting someone who was so good and loved us so much?

I felt powerless to stop Jeff's decline and I became very angry with God for the pain we were going through. Throughout the spring and summer of 1974, I spent less and less time at home, unable to stand it anymore, and a bit more time doing things I probably shouldn't have, like smoking the occasional joint. A couple of years earlier, at age fifteen, I had smoked marijuana for the first time at a rock concert. As my friends and I sat in the massive Barton Coliseum and felt the beat of the music pounding through us, someone began passing around a marijuana cigarette. I took a drag, and settled back to feel the effects of the drug. The music seemed to become even louder, and I felt relaxed, at ease. Although I didn't know it at the time, I had taken a critical first step.

Bill, still teaching at the University of Arkansas in Fayetteville, was also running for Congress. In the primary race that spring he beat back challenges from three opponents, then won a runoff election, earning the right to challenge the incumbent, Congressman John Paul Hammerschmidt.

Hammerschmidt was a heavily entrenched Republican who represented the northwestern portion of Arkansas. He was considered unbeatable and hadn't faced a tough political opponent since first winning his seat in 1966. A wealthy businessman from

Harrison, located in the north central part of the state, Hammerschmidt built a solid record of constituent service. Nonetheless, Bill decided he wanted to mount a challenge to the congressman. My brother climbed into his 1970 AMC Gremlin and began campaigning through Hammerschmidt's district. "I just jumped in my little car and had a helluva time," he said of the experience.

Mother and I had a hell of a time, too. We enjoyed campaigning for Bill; putting up posters, handing out literature, talking with friends. Jeff went to Fayetteville and worked for a few weeks in Bill's campaign headquarters until his health forced him to return home. Bill still insists that the 1974 campaign is the best one he's ever run. It was our first real effort as a political family, and we almost won the election. In fact, we went to bed on election night believing we *had* won. Bill gave Congressman Hammerschmidt a real scare, but lost the race by something like 4 percent of the vote.

One afternoon in August, I was at home with Jeff, but leaving soon to go out with friends and anxious to make sure he was going to be okay alone until my mother came home. Jeff went into the bedroom without the phone to take a nap; in his own bedroom, he was often awakened by the phone next to his bed.

I helped him get into bed and sat there beside him for a few moments talking quietly to him. He told me again how much he loved me. Mother, I mentioned to him, was coming home with barbecue for dinner. Would he mind, I asked, if I went to shoot pool with my friends for an hour or so, then come home for dinner?

"Son," he told me, "you go shoot pool. I'll be fine. I'm just going to lie here and take a little nap. When your mother gets home, we'll eat dinner."

I went to the bowling alley and played pool with my friends, maybe bowled a game, too. A little over an hour later when I returned home, Jeff was dead.

When I drove up to the house, I noticed the Frasers' car in our driveway. They were neighbors who lived just two houses up the street, and in all the years we'd known them, this was the first time they had driven down to our house—usually they walked.

Mr. Fraser met me at the door. "Roger," he said, "I'm so sorry."

"Where's Mother?" I demanded, pushing my way past him. I came around the corner and saw my mother standing a few feet away, crying softly. "Mr. Fraser," I asked, my voice rising, "what are y'all doing here?"

"Roger," Mother said quietly, "Jeff's gone."

I couldn't accept it. I didn't understand.

"What do you mean, gone?" I asked, incredulous.

The guilt and regret slammed home. If I had been there, if I had stayed, maybe something would be different.

Mother, still crying, told me she had come home and found Jeff dead. The bedcovers were still arranged just as they had been when I left. He hadn't even moved. He had just fallen asleep.

I blamed myself because Mother had been the one to find Jeff, not me. She had come home with a barbecue dinner and had called to Jeff from the kitchen. She knew Jeff would be sleeping, and thought little of it when he didn't answer her call. When she went back to wake him up for dinner, she found him dead.

I didn't blame myself for Jeff's death, but I blamed myself for letting him die alone. And I blamed God. The pain and fear had come back into our lives, and again I blamed God for allowing it all to happen again.

I turned to go out driving, but our neighbor Rose Crane wouldn't let me go alone. She drove while I cried. It just wasn't fair, losing two fathers.

Bill delivered the eulogy at Jeff's funeral service. "I can honestly say I never knew a better man," he said of Jeff.

Jeff's death had an even more devastating effect on Mother. It made her wonder, simply enough, if she were really meant to be married. She had lost Bill's father in an auto accident two months before Bill was born; she lost my father to alcohol and cancer, and now she'd lost Jeff as well.

"Nothing good comes easy," Mother always told me. But where was the good in this?

In retrospect, I thank God for putting Jeff Dwire in my life and for allowing him to pass away so peacefully. Considering the alternative—the nightmare of hospitals, machines and tubes—I'm glad he died so quietly.

Would my life have been otherwise if Jeff had lived a little longer? He died about the time I turned eighteen—a critical age for any young person, especially one growing up in the turbulent 1970s. Perhaps if he'd been around I might have viewed the world a little differently over the next few years, but I'm not sure.

CHAPTER TWO

THE LONG AND WINDING ROAD

I had begun to get into trouble even before Jeff's death in 1974. More importantly to me, however, I also began to get into music. I was sixteen when I began singing in Hot Springs nightclubs, although I'd been singing all my life in church and to Mother in the early morning hours while she got ready for work. She particularly liked "Red Roses for a Blue Lady."

As a youngster, I'd spent a lot of time with my friend Steve Housley, who lived down the block from us on Scully Street. Steve's dad, Charley, would take us on hunting and camping trips. Charley was an impressive guy—there wasn't much he couldn't do. He and his brother were in the roofing business, but their talent didn't stop there. Charley built cabin cruisers, put together jeeps from spare parts, and he'd once been an auctioneer. He loved country-and-western music, and he'd performed with several small country bands. In the back room of his house, he had a small amplifier and an old microphone. I would go over to Charley's and sing, with Charley sort of coaching me along.

"Gentle on My Mind" was his particular favorite, and he asked me to sing the song often. He was the first person outside my family who gave me the encouragement to follow a career in music.

I followed Charley's direction because, until Jeff Dwire came along, Charley had been something of a father to me. At times, when my father was drunk, Charley would stand between us. I worshiped Charley, and I'll be forever grateful he led me toward music as a career.

Early on, as a freshman in high school, I experimented with a couple of different bands before finally settling into one, Dealer's Choice. The other members of Dealer's Choice were outstanding musicians. Paul Chunn was on drums and he had a strong singing voice. I have a good range, but Paul could easily top me. His talent was always evident when we sang Grand Funk-style harmony. Steve Roach played lead guitar and, from time to time, he'd sit down at the keyboard. Vaughan Reed was our bass player.

We tried several times to add a keyboardist, but to no avail. Several trouped in and out of the band—Larry Minnie and Larry Satterly come to mind. Kenny Hall from Benton became our new drummer when the traveling became too much of a strain for Paul Chunn. Paul had a chronic heart condition and he couldn't leave town to play the dates we'd booked. We added Johnny Jones, a neighbor of Kenny Hall's, as a second guitarist. This five-piece band stayed together for the next several years and continued to play gigs even after I went off to college. At first, we mostly played in Hot Springs nightclubs, such as the Black Orchid. The Club Car was one of the lounges I played in, down on Central Avenue. We appeared at Holiday Inn's Finish Line Lounge, the Derby Show Lounge, and later, Tiffany's. Starting out, we played mainly during race meets, when the town was packed every night. People and horses would begin arriving right after Christmas to work out on the track a month or two before the races began in February.

The trackers wanted to hear country-and-western music, while most of our stuff was Top 40 rock and roll. Looking back, I can't blame them. Our music was mechanical and lacked any innovation. We sounded like *everybody* else, just another band knocking off "MacArthur Park."

Then there were the brawls. The trainers, hot walkers, jockeys, grooms—the folks on the back side that were the heart of racing—worked long days and would come in for a few beers and some dancing, ready to unwind and let their hair down. One club, Tiffany's, held about a thousand people and we could count on a fight breaking out like clockwork. It was not rare for the participants to end up in our laps in the middle of a set.

As we gained experience and our reputation spread, the band would travel to Little Rock and Fayetteville, even out of state. We'd play conventions and school dances. My appearances with the band took up most of my weekends for seven years, but I didn't mind. I was grateful for the opportunity to work with my friends, and I loved being in front of a crowd— still do. It goes to show that if you have a dream, pursue it, and never give up, you'll eventually get where you want to go.

By the time I began singing professionally, Jeff was too ill to come to the nightclubs and watch me perform. Nonetheless, he encouraged Mother to take her friends along to hear me sing. Jeff thought the family should do everything it could to support me, even if he couldn't show up himself.

My mother would come in with one of her friends, usually Nancy Crawford Adkins or Ann Tyler. They were my fan club. Their cheering might have seemed loud or silly to some, but I loved having them there. I'd give anything if Mother could come and watch me perform in concert settings today. At least she saw me perform at the close of the Democratic National Convention, when Bill was nominated for the presidency.

The band was my life during high school, but I had always planned to go to college to study communications, with an eye towards becoming a sports broadcaster. I had been considering Louisiana State University's journalism department, or—perhaps the better choice—the University of Missouri at Columbia. As it turned out, I didn't even get across the state line. Jeff died in August 1974. When he passed away, I decided I wasn't going anywhere. Mother had lost two husbands in my memory—three if you count Bill's father, Bill Blythe. I made up my mind I wasn't going to leave her alone. I would stay at home, take care of her, and be the man of the house. "End of discussion," I told Bill and Mother, "I'm staying here. I'll get a job and help pay the bills."

But my resolve didn't hold, and Mother and Bill wanted me to go ahead and go to college. "I'll compromise," I told them, "I'll go somewhere here in Arkansas." A college in Arkansas wasn't my second choice; it had never been an option. I believe the colleges and universities in Arkansas are excellent, but I had always wanted to go out of state.

By the time Mother and Bill had convinced me to get on with my freshman year, most of the institutions in Arkansas had already started classes. Here, fate stepped in—in the person of Tim Brooks, who had been my friend for years.

Tim's family owned a beautiful religious retreat in Hot Springs. He had attended the rival junior high school—Central, where Bill had gone. Tim was always a very religious person, and he suggested I go to Hendrix, a private Methodist school in Conway, Arkansas.

⊷ THE HARVARD OF ARKANSAS ⊷

Tim knew I needed some stability, and he worked hard to convince me to take a look at Hendrix. Because the school operated on a three-semester annual calendar, classes hadn't yet begun for the fall term. I went up to Conway, looked around Hendrix, and liked what I saw. Tim, who was planning to major in theology, sealed the deal by asking me to be his roommate.

You know, many college roommates end up hating each other; but today, Tim and I are still very good friends. We saw each other not long ago at our twentieth high school reunion, and we had a great visit talking over old times. He and his family still run Brookhill Ranch, now the premier facility of its kind in that part of the country.

I left for my freshman year at Hendrix College in Conway just a few weeks after Jeff had died. Still devastated by the loss, the excitement and challenge of entering college gave me something to occupy my mind and my time.

At Hendrix, we didn't have fraternities, and campus life was defined by the dormitories. Martin Hall was home to a lot of jocks and party people. We wore our hair long and were somewhat unruly, amusing ourselves by terrorizing others with our high jinks. We'd dump trash in the hallways, bomb open windows with water balloons, streak, and just generally play at going to college. At least three times a week, we'd go out, drive around, or hang out at the lake drinking wine—the good stuff, Boone's Farm, Strawberry Hill, and Apple.

I enrolled in a terrific honors composition class, which allowed me to work on my writing skills. Since there was no journalism curriculum, I chose Western Civilization, American History, Russian History, and a class called Communism, Fascism and Democracy. These last two were heady stuff for me, especially as the Cold War was still raging. Regardless of how fascinating the material, these subjects weren't what I wanted to study. I realize now, my first year at Hendrix was a complete and total test of my will to be there in the first place.

Once I had enrolled in those freshman courses, Tim and I set out to explore our new domain of Conway, Arkansas. At that time, the town was home to two colleges—Hendrix and the University of Central Arkansas, our cross-town rival. With a population of about twenty-five thousand, Conway also had one AM radio station, a quaint—and compared to Hot Springs, quiet—downtown section, and dozens of fast-food restaurants all catering to the college crowd.

To reach Conway from Hot Springs, you could either drive to Little Rock and head back west for about thirty miles, or head north to Russellville and then turn east on the interstate for a forty-minute drive. I wore grooves in both routes, returning home almost every weekend to make sure Mother was getting along all right. At home alone now, she at least had her anesthesiology practice, which was going well. Bill was still teaching at the University and he'd drive down from Fayetteville quite often to see her, also. Together, they'd go out at night, sit in the nightclubs and listen to music. Bill said Mother seemed to be on "automatic pilot" during that time.

On Mondays, I'd get back to business. Hendrix has the justified reputation for being one of the state's toughest schools academically, and in Conway and elsewhere around Arkansas it is often referred to as "Little Harvard." It was a challenging time for me, juggling a heavy class load with the demands of my music and an active social life. Needless to say, I did not devote as much time to my studies as I should have.

By the time the spring trimester had come to an end in early June, two monumental events were taking place in my life: I had nearly decided not to come back to school for another year; instead, I would "lay out" a year and focus on my music. Also, Bill was getting married.

➤ MEETING HILLARY ➤

I first met Hillary Rodham in New Haven on a visit to Bill. Small-town sixteen-year-old that I was, I thought her hair was silly and hated her coke-bottle glasses. Mother and I looked at her, then looked at each other, surprised, because Bill usually dated Barbie doll types. Hillary was different, indeed.

For starters, she was brilliant. And, she already knew Bill was going to be in her life. Frankly, I was jealous of her.

During their courtship, Hillary and I would rarely get together, mainly because Bill wasn't living in Hot Springs anymore. When they did come to visit, Big Brother would bridge conversational gaps and generally smooth things over. I felt intimidated by Hillary, by her straightforwardness and independence. Even then, she was very aware, very worldly.

Mother and I weren't convinced they were going to walk into the sunset, but it didn't take long to see their real connection to one another. Bill left us no doubt that Hillary made him happy, and that had to be good enough for us. So we tolerated Hillary before real fondness set in.

My own problems with Hillary stemmed largely from *my* problems with *myself.* As I hit bottom and began to recover some years later, my self-image began to improve, and my relationship with Hillary changed along with my perception of myself.

But losing Bill to someone else? The family had always been me, Big Brother, and Mother, I thought to myself. Now, Hillary

Rodham was in the picture. I guess at first I didn't believe they would actually end up getting married.

The wedding took place in October 1975. I was Bill's best man, but I can't remember much of the ceremony because I was too busy feeling sorry for myself.

My mother was at the wedding, of course. Hillary's parents and her two brothers, Hugh and Tony, both students at the University of Arkansas, were also there.

Bill and Hillary exchanged heirloom rings. Everything was over except for the shouting—Bill had invited about two hundred friends and political supporters to a reception the day after the wedding. One of the guests was Arkansas Attorney General Jim Guy Tucker, who succeeded Bill as governor when he resigned to move to Washington in early 1993.

Tucker had encouraged Bill to seek the attorney general's position, but Bill hadn't yet made up his mind. At the reception, he told the members of the press who were there that he'd run for something in 1976, but he wasn't sure what. His options were pretty much limited to attorney general or mounting another challenge against Congressman Hammerschmidt.

Bill and Hillary purchased a home in Fayetteville, just at the end of Fraternity Row on the University of Arkansas campus. It looked charming from the outside, but the interior was utter chaos. It had a big fireplace, basement, high ceilings, and wood floors, and was the kind of house he'd grown up in; the kind of house we both loved. "This is what's so great, Rog," he would tell me as he pointed out the features of the home. The interior needed a lot of work and required vision. Bill and Hillary did the work and supplied the vision, creating a beautiful home.

⤠ WAFFLING ⤟

I called a family meeting to discuss taking a year off from school. The decision called for a vote. "I'm not a quitter," I told them, as I sat at the end of the table and watched their faces, "I just need time to play my music and think." When we voted—with the three of us, there were never any ties—Mother wanted me to return to Hendrix and pursue my degree, but Bill apparently thought I ought to do what made me happy and he voted with me. I promised I would eventually return to Hendrix, and I did. But right then, in the summer of 1975, I wanted to get back to the band. Bill later said, "I kind of thought Roger was wasting his life. But he probably thought I was wasting mine."

Almost as soon as I'd made the decision to leave Hendrix for a year and concentrate on my music, our band bookings began to pick up. By this time, we were fairly well-known across the state; the make-up of the band was consistent, our music kept improving, and we were in steady demand.

During that year away from Hendrix, I experimented with drugs. I wasn't using anything on a regular or heavy basis; drugs were merely recreational, and I indulged only every now and then. However, the frequency of my "experimentations" began to increase.

As I promised Mother and Bill, I returned to Hendrix in the fall of 1976. By then, Bill had been elected attorney general.

Arkansas was still a one-party state, and no Republican candidate challenged my brother in the fall election. I helped him campaign during the primary race that spring, hammering yard signs into the ground by the hundreds.

Bill was sworn into office as attorney general in January 1977. At Hendrix, I was about forty miles away from his office in Little Rock and I drove down to see him as often as I could.

That second year at school, I lived about a mile off campus with two roommates. My classes were more varied, more intense, and consequently required more of me. I took International Relations and helped with the Arkansas Model United Nations across town at the University of Central Arkansas. That's where I met Jim Moore, friend and author, for the first time. Jim told me later that he thought I had the world on the downhill pull.

That might have been true, but not in the way Jim meant. My second year at Hendrix was largely wasted time for me. I spent most of my non-class hours listening to music instead of studying—Todd Rundgren, the Moody Blues, and the Beatles.

At the close of my sophomore year at Hendrix, I decided to go back to the band—again. This time, though, I laid out of college for two years. My use of drugs became more and more frequent, and the music became less and less important. I traveled a great deal with the band, but the music gradually became a sideline to the drugs rather than the other way around. Bill ran for governor in 1978, and when he won the election that fall, my world changed.

I just wasn't mature enough to handle being the brother of the man who ran the state. The Arkansas press had a good time with me, reporting what I did, the social functions I attended, where I went. When I was in Arkansas, I lived here and there— I spent some time at Mother's, and I stayed at the Governor's Mansion when I was in Little Rock. It was, after all, my brother's house, and in my flawed reasoning, I judged it was my house as well.

When Hillary and Big Brother moved into the Mansion, I was welcome to stay at the guest house, which was set apart from the main house. I'd come through the gate, greet the guards, park, and settle in. Sometimes a friend or two was with me and there were times I was hammered, just stoned out of my head. Generally, Bill and Hillary were already asleep when I wandered in, but of course they caught on.

Hillary once admonished me, "Roger, you will not come here anymore and stay at the Governor's Mansion without calling first. I realize he's your brother, but this is not your home. At least respect us enough to call."

Her tone was not angry. She was matter-of-fact, but very compelling. For me, it should have been a wake-up call, but I'm not sure it accomplished much.

In the late summer of 1979, Hillary told us she was pregnant. The baby was expected around mid-March, but Chelsea came a bit early in February 1980. Her birth was a wonderful event, and even though I was using drugs rather heavily at the time and wasn't in the best frame of mind, I was elated at the prospect of being an uncle. I remember Bill coming out to the waiting area about 1:30 in the morning to introduce us to his daughter.

Mother had always wanted a little girl, and now she had a beautiful granddaughter.

➤❦ DOWNHILL AND ACCELERATING ❦◄

Although the initial year of my brother's first term as governor had gone well enough, Chelsea's birth was one of the few bright spots of the second year. In most respects, 1980 was an unmitigated disaster. Every time we turned around, something went wrong. The summer of 1980, Jimmy Carter sent hundreds of Cuban refugees to Fort Chaffee, near Fort Smith, Arkansas. The Cubans rioted, and Bill was blamed for letting Carter get away with sending the Cubans to us. My brother's Republican challenger, Frank White, promised to repeal the car-tag fee increase enacted during the Clinton administration. The summer drought was particularly bad, and the state's poultry industry suffered. A Titan II missile blew up in its Arkansas silo. There were some minor scandals within the state government. None of this was my brother's fault, but that didn't matter.

As we campaigned that summer, the entire family could feel the election slipping away, but there was nothing we could do to stop it. While the political pundits were still predicting an easy Clinton victory, we weren't deluded. I remember watching challenger Frank White on television that election night, rebel-yelling with elation over upsetting my brother.

Bill, Hillary, and Chelsea moved out of the Mansion, and the White family moved in. My brother found a quaint yellow house in a section of Little Rock called "The Heights"— a district of mostly historic homes. The house had old-fashioned high ceilings and a library big enough for even Bill and Hillary's massive book collection. Bill went into private law practice with Bruce Lindsey and seemed quite content. The election, it turned out, had taught him a lesson he might not have learned any other way. Bill vowed never again to lose the common touch, to let people know what he was doing, and to find out what their needs were. When he was ready to launch his 1982 comeback bid, he'd coined the philosophy into a slogan: "You can't lead without listening." As it turned out, Arkansans were receptive to his message after two years of Frank White.

As Bill entered the 1982 gubernatorial primaries, I entered the world of narcotics commerce and dealt drugs for three years before my arrest. During most of that time, Bill was governor of the state. Having such a popular and powerful brother was a wonderful experience even under the circumstances; I just wish I had been clear-headed enough to really enjoy it.

⇥ DEALING BIG-TIME ⇤

Years ago I dabbled exclusively in marijuana. I never saw anything wrong with it—marijuana made me happy and hungry. Then came cocaine.

It was easy enough to fall into and it quickly became a full-fledged addiction. Anyone who watches an addiction develop has seen how predictable stupid behaviors are; in fact, the only to do drug deals. After making the transaction, I'd spend several days relaxing at racetracks and having fun. When I was back home, I hung out at Oaklawn racetrack, traveled around with the band a bit, and often stayed with friends on Lake Hamilton or at Mother's lake house. I had a little one-person speed boat that was about half the size of a regular boat and weighed maybe sixty pounds. It had a forty-five-horsepower outboard on the back end, and that baby would fly over the waves, leaping five or six feet into the air as I topped the crests. The danger never seemed to matter to me at the time.

I may have been oblivious, but I'm not so sure Mother was. I recall one incident in particular that may have aroused her suspicions. Years earlier, Mother and Jeff had given me a 1967 Mustang convertible, and throughout my late teens and twenties I spent thousands of nights bopping around in the Mustang with the top down. One particular night in 1984, however, I drove quietly home with the top buttoned up. The convertible top, which Mother had just replaced for me, was ripped down the middle, torn by a violent knife gash. Someone must have vandalized the car while I was inside a Hot Springs nightclub, I told Mother. It wasn't the whole truth, but she moved to call the police and the insurance carrier. I stopped her. Baffled, she gave me a long look and shrugged her shoulders.

What I didn't tell her, and what I didn't want the police to know, was that I'd had cocaine in the car. Someone had stolen the stuff before I could deliver it, and now I owed my supplier eight thousand dollars.

person blind to them is the addict. During my own downward spiral, I was introduced to a guy from Columbia who became my partner in dealing.

Initially, I had to deal with the fear of moving through airports with ounces and ounces of coke on my person—coke in my socks, in my underwear, in jacket pockets. At first the metal detector spooked me so my partner and I practiced the first few runs. To put me at ease, he carried the drugs and I carried nothing.

My first solo pass through the detector was a nightmare. When I came upon it, my nerve failed and I turned to a newsstand for something to read, paid for it, and pocketed my change. Once again I approached the detector when it dawned on me that my change might trigger the mechanism. Panicked, I returned to the store and gave the change back to the clerk. "Here, take this. I don't want it," I said, then walked out.

Things were moving in slow motion. I was about five feet behind a woman just passing through the detector. As I stepped nearer, the beeper went off and I was convinced it had found me out. But three people were striding up to the woman, and a guard was signaling me through. I balked again, then gritted my teeth and went on. No buzzer went off, and I was home free. The process became easier and easier as my addiction increased. Eventually, I did the majority of my dealing during cold months in cold climates so I could conceal more of the drug in bulky winter clothing.

For a good deal of Bill's second term, I stayed out of Arkansas, flying to New York, California, Kentucky, and Florida

I've done a lot of thinking about the forces that drove me not only to use drugs, but to sell them. I could blame many things, but the bottom line is I was really screwed up inside.

Drugs were carrying me away. Music was the front—the excuse I needed to travel all over the country. Then I would sit back and party between deals. Since my expenses were low I did not need much money to live on and I had only to worry about the next deal. It was an awful way to live, and I know now how lucky I was to have survived it all. Near the end, I begged internally for it all to be over. Soon enough, I would get my wish.

CHAPTER THREE

SHUTTING THE GATES BEHIND

Any summer in Hot Springs, Arkansas, is hot and sticky, especially in July. The mornings are heavy with humidity, and I awoke one day weighed down with the apprehension that something bad was going to happen.

It was the summer of 1984, the year of my twenty-eighth birthday, and I had driven the few miles' distance to my Mother's rural home to feed her dogs while she was away for the day. As I turned off the main road and onto the country lane that led to her driveway, I passed a strange sight out in the middle of nowhere—a big, dark sedan. I pulled into my mother's driveway, got out, unlocked her front door, and went inside.

The dogs were in the back yard. There was King, a black-and-silver German shepherd who was my best friend growing up, and my mother's chow, Ching. Both greeted me with their usual burst of affection as I went about the business of scooping dog food into their dishes. Just as I set their dishes down on the floor there was a knock at the front door. Opening it, I stood

face-to-face with two state police officers who identified themselves as agents with the state's drug enforcement task force. My
two years of drug dealing had suddenly come to an end.

There are people who can do something wrong with the
arrogant assumption they'll never have to pay the piper, although
such was never the case with me. I always assumed that, sooner or
later, I'd get caught, especially recently, as tip-offs from friends
and contacts in Hot Springs and Little Rock had become com-
monplace. Apparently, some sort of big investigation was underway, and a couple of individuals involved in drug traffic had told
the officers what they knew. Despite my friends' warnings that I
was a suspect, I kept dealing drugs, only at a much slower pace.
Unfortunately, the drug had a hold on me, and while I might have
left dealing behind, I couldn't do without the drug.

As we walked into my mother's living room and sat down,
they asked me if I knew why they had come to see me. I told them
I thought I did.

As they arrested me and apprised me of my rights I began
to cry. The tears came not so much for fear of what might happen to Roger Clinton but out of a tremendous sense of relief—
relief that the long-dreaded confrontation with the authorities
was finally happening.

The officers were there to do a job and they began asking me
questions about my friends, contacts, and suppliers in the drug
business. I answered their questions, usually giving them the
wrong answers. My cocaine habit had screwed up my head—right
was wrong and wrong was right. The cops were the enemy, and I

only wanted to protect my "friends." I could not know it yet, but this entire experience would help me learn an important lesson—real, honest friends are tough to come by. Many of the "friends" I sought to protect would desert me when I went to trial and on to prison.

Gandhi once said that if you knew how, you could even find a way out of hell. For me, someone was pointing the way. The officers were using their considerable powers of persuasion to show me how I could shorten my prison sentence. If I cooperated with the state and turned in my friends, the officers told me, it would help me in court.

They produced a document stating I wouldn't contact anyone else being investigated and asked me to sign it. The officers were probably watching most of my friends, intent on arresting most of them in a few days' time. I felt completely powerless and was, in fact, in no position to decline the requests of the state police. I signed.

Released on my own recognizance, I watched impassively as they got into their unmarked car, backed out of the driveway, and headed back up the road towards town. Immediately, I dove for the telephone and called my friends.

"They're on to you," I told them. Most of them reacted with the same lackadaisical attitude I had when friends had repeated the exact words to me, telling me not to worry. Easy for them to say—they hadn't been arrested yet.

I had made a promise to the officers, and sealed it with my signature, pledging on my sacred honor I would not contact my friends. But because I was so sick—because of the hold my cocaine habit had on me—I saw the situation as honorable treachery and felt no remorse about breaking my word.

⇤ THINKING AND TALKING SUICIDE ⇥

That afternoon, I wrestled with the enormous implications of what had just happened. The officers had assured me that if I failed to cooperate with them, I would go to prison for a long time. However, from the outset, I felt that even if I *did* cooperate, I would still go to jail. The question was, for how long?

During the next few days, I began to have self-pitying thoughts about suicide. Pacing back and forth, I pondered the mess I was in, trying to find a quick and easy way out. That was, after all, the Roger Clinton modus operandi—a quick and easy way out. At least it was for the Roger Clinton on drugs. Besides, if I killed myself, my mother and my brother would be spared the agony of seeing me sent to prison.

I always thought that suicide was something weak people did, other people who didn't have the genuine, supportive love of a family, or who were pitiful souls with low self-esteem, overwhelmed by life's pressures. How wrong I was. I was considering suicide despite the fact that I had a mother and older brother who deeply loved me.

For the next few days, the dogs and the telephone my constant companions, I hung around my mother's house calling friends to tell them I had been arrested. It wasn't long before the anticipated family showdown, when I would for the first time tell Bill and Mother about my suicidal thoughts, took place.

The encounter was heated and emotional. They knew something was up and were positioned around the room, expecting the worst. I really let them have it.

"I'm going to kill myself."

At the time, we were in the living room with Mother on the sofa and Bill sitting across from me at the table. Mother was already crying, but she began to sob almost uncontrollably after I uttered those words.

I was delirious and ticked off at the world, crying and sweating so hard my hair was soaked. Frantic about my situation and scared, I must have been incomprehensible. I looked at Big Brother. "I'm just not going to put you through the pain and embarrassment of having a brother like me."

"And how do you propose to do that?" Bill yelled back at me, leaning forward in his seat to put his face into mine.

"I'm going to kill myself!" I screamed back. "Look what I've done to you and Mother, the two most important people in the world to me!"

All of a sudden, Bill reached out, grabbed me by the upper arm and started shaking me violently. I was as scared as I've ever been in my life and I know I was blabbering on incoherently, barely able to see through my tears.

"You're sick," he finally told me, his voice dripping with scorn.

The next thing I knew, he was shaking me by the shoulders, shoving me back and forth while he yelled at me, his reddened face just inches from mine.

"How dare you be so selfish! You're the most precious thing in the world to your mother and me, and you'd dare think about taking that away from us?"

Bill was furious. His face was beet red, with tears streaming down his cheeks and over his lips. I had never seen him that angry before, and I think it's safe to say I'll never see him that angry again. His anger terrified me.

This was a moment of truth, beginning with my admission that I wanted to kill myself, then spilling my guts to him. I had been keeping secrets about my sordid life from him and now finally I was coming clean. It wasn't so much that I had been lying outright to him and Mother—it was more a matter of concealing the truth. That was how I rationalized it, anyway.

Bill was livid, but I sensed that he, too, was as scared as he was angry. His voice trembled as he spoke to me, trying first to reason with me and then consoling me as only he could. I was his little brother but he had always taken care of me. Bill had always been very possessive and protective, my only real father figure. This encounter shocked him into realizing how close he was to losing me, but what concerned him more than his loss of me were my self-destructive tendencies, my decline into a cocaine addition, the possibility that I would waste my life.

Finally, he stopped shaking me, but he kept both hands on my shoulders. I looked into his eyes and saw the hurt, the anger, and the raw emotion he felt. Bill's rage shocked me, and I was crying, too, because I hadn't expected this sort of violent response.

"Don't worry so much about what other people will think of your life," Bill said, as we all started to calm down a bit. "You need to be accountable to yourself. You would be cheating yourself with suicide."

Bill saved my life that day. He hung in there with me, working through the fear and the anger to reassure me I had a commitment to myself. Only later in life did I realize that Bill was bearing a lot of my guilt because he believed he had somehow failed me.

As he talked, he reminisced about those times in our lives when he had let me down in some way. He eventually admitted he had sheltered me too much, hoping things were hunky-dory because I was making decent grades in school, when in fact I was acting up in school, making a regular nuisance of myself around authority figures.

As I discovered in subsequent counseling, you have to think of yourself. Not just the consequences of your behavior on others, but the consequences of what you do to yourself because no one will do it for you. A drug addict is never actually healed: You're either a practicing addict or a recovering addict. It's a simple choice, and if you face that, accept that, and not run from the stigma of being an "ex-addict," you can deal with your life.

Thank goodness my brother was there—and not a gun. I was not thinking very clearly at the time, and who knows what I would have done with a gun in my hand?

The balance of our family meeting was matter-of-fact, given the circumstances. Bill did not reveal to me at the time that he had known of my impending arrest weeks before the officers moved in. As sick as I was, I would have felt anger and resentment if I *had* known—and did, when I found out later. Bill recommended a lawyer in a Little Rock law firm, and I followed up on his advice.

Throughout our long conversation in the living room, Mother had behaved a bit more predictably. When I told her I had been arrested she put her arms around me and hugged me. "We've climbed mountains before," she told me. "We've got one more to climb."

The trail ahead looked pretty dark just then. I would have to struggle through one day at a time, and what bothered me most was the uncertainty—the dread of prison, the fear of what would happen next, and the worry about how my arrest would affect my brother's political career. At the same time, I was struggling to wean my body away from the half-dozen grams of cocaine—each dose enough to kill a man—I had been doing each day.

The time between my arrest and trial was tortuous. I'm certain I couldn't have survived it without the support of my family and a few friends, as well as the love of God.

ICED

My arrest in 1984 was one thing, but being restricted and harassed by the state police was another. They visited me daily, sometimes catching me on the street and hustling me into their unmarked sedans. I was wired for sound to catch other suspected drug dealers in the act of incriminating themselves, but time after time, I tipped suspects off with facial expressions, ruining the setup.

Each time, the troopers figured out what I was doing and they'd get pissed off. At times, they threatened that they would somehow do away with me, and no one would ever see or hear from me again. That, I was told repeatedly, would be the penalty if I did not cooperate. So there I was, threatened by the same people hired to protect and serve. I didn't know who the bad guys were.

I was taken to a dank Hot Springs hotel room, where the officers arranged polygraph examinations. I failed the test multiple times.

"You're making fools of us," the officers charged, "You're trying to make us look like idiots."

Invariably, such statements would be followed by the threat that I was going to prison for a long, long time. Or, if I didn't cooperate, people might never see me again. "Even if you're not found guilty in court," the officers told me, "you're still going to prison."

What bothered me most was the constant verbal abuse. The officers spoke to me as if I were the worst sort of trash and predicted dire consequences for me if I continued to lead them on wild goose chases.

My initial decision not to cooperate with the investigating officers was solidified by the treatment I received from one state trooper. Ironically, this was a trooper assigned to Bill's security staff during his first term as governor, and at that time he seemed to enjoy driving me and my friends to official functions. Prior to the arrest, the trooper proclaimed he thought the world of me, and I considered him a good friend. Now, with the situation so radically altered, he would shove me up against his car and tell me I was nothing but a low-life, and that no matter who my brother was, I was in trouble.

Finally, I decided I had taken enough. One night when I was at the Governor's Mansion, I telephoned Tommy Goodwin, the head of the Arkansas State Police.

I had never met Colonel Goodwin before, and I introduced myself to him over the telephone. I explained that my life was being threatened, and he replied, "Give me their names. Those are the guys we're looking for."

"No sir," I responded, "You don't understand. My life is being threatened by your men. I'm not scared of the other side. I'm scared of your side. Your side is supposed to protect and serve. That's the side I'm afraid of."

"I can't believe the gall you have," my brother told me when I informed him of the call.

My call to Colonel Goodwin must have succeeded; the abusive trooper was reassigned. I later learned the trooper's odd behavior stemmed from the fact that he was not rehired as one of the members of my brother's security team after Bill defeated Frank White in their 1982 rematch. Apparently, he became very bitter towards my family in general, and my brother in particular.

Because of Colonel Goodwin's intervention on my behalf, I decided to plead guilty to the charges against me, and not to flee the country. Leaving the United States had certainly been an option, although it wasn't a particularly attractive one. I'd have to sneak back into the country to see my family and would likely be on the run for the rest of my life. My drug-dealing partner had urged me to fly with him to Bogota, Colombia, where he said we could live with his mother and father. While the thought of starting a new life in Colombia held some fleeting appeal, I was finally beginning to think a bit more clearly. I discussed the option with Bill, and he convinced me that leaving the country would be foolish.

"Go do your prison time," Bill told me, "and get your life back together."

Eventually, the state police abandoned their efforts to use me as an informant in their investigation. Trooper Mike Mahone from Jacksonville was assigned to my case, and within two weeks of my call to Colonel Goodwin, the harassment, threats, and verbal abuse abruptly ceased. Strangely enough, this decision to leave me alone only served to intensify my sense of isolation. As a hot July melted into an equally oppressive August, I figured the best thing I could do was to get back to life as usual. Several years earlier, I had attended Hendrix College in Conway, Arkansas, on and off for a few years, dropping out before I obtained my degree. Now, it seemed logical to resume my college career. I hoped that going to classes and studying would help take my mind off the daily uncertainty that dogged me.

Part of the problem with returning to college was that the Arkansas press was dogging my every move with unrelenting tenacity. Articles about my arrest and impending court battle appeared almost every day in the two Little Rock newspapers.

The media's interest in me quickened as the fall elections drew nearer. Not that my situation—and Bill's—wasn't ripe for attention. He was tackling his own political struggle head-on, and here comes Little Brother, rattling a large skeleton from the closet. What better fodder for the press? In the end, though, they underestimated my brother and overestimated the depth of the public's interest in what had happened to me.

My life was in a state of flux. My case was proceeding through the justice system, my friends were changing, my daily routine had been dramatically altered, even my hairstyle was different. Before my arrest, I looked like a rock musician, with hair down past my shoulders. Afterwards, I cut it short and tried to look like a normal, upstanding citizen, even if I wasn't, quite.

⇒ BACK TO SCHOOL ⇐

I returned to Hendrix for my senior year. It wasn't an easy road to take—I had already completed all the easier courses, and had to sign up for the most difficult upper-level classes.

At first, the administrators at Hendrix welcomed me back with open arms. My brother drove with me from Little Rock to Conway to visit with the deans of the college and to argue my case before them. One of them, John Churchill, was a long-time friend of Bill's and a fellow Rhodes scholar. I was well enough, Bill told them, to come back to school, to study and to work hard.

We told the deans my trial date had been set: I would go before a judge in January 1985. The impending trial—and the media coverage that was bound to ensue—didn't seem to concern the assembled deans, who agreed to take me back.

I tried my best to integrate myself into school life, living close to campus in Conway. Then, as my brother's campaign organization began to worry about my accessibility to the press, I moved to Little Rock, where I had a small apartment overlooking the Arkansas River. My proximity to the press was no less, but perhaps they felt they could control things better if I was closer to headquarters. Daily, I commuted back and forth to Conway— an eighty-mile round trip.

Although I had been away from college for three years and had all these other distractions hanging over my head, I managed to do well, earning a 3.0 grade point average. I even tried to involve myself in intramural sports and regularly played organized touch football.

During one of these touch football games, one of the players on the field suffered a broken collarbone. I had nothing to do with the accident; in fact, I helped load the young man in the car for the short drive to the hospital. It had been raining in Conway, the field was wet, and the player simply slipped. But some misunderstanding occurred and two students I didn't know told the administration I was responsible for the accident. The deans mentioned the incident among themselves, but said nothing about it to me until later.

Despite incidents like this one, my first two months at Hendrix were calm and quiet. I made new friends in Conway, kept my grades up, and maintained a positive attitude, trying hard not to worry about my upcoming trial or what others thought about me.

Interesting things always seem to happen on Halloween. For instance, Harry Houdini died on that day in 1926. October 31, 1984, was a Wednesday. That was the day I was called into the dean's office and given an option to voluntarily withdraw from Hendrix or face expulsion.

The news hit me like a thunderbolt. It didn't make any sense. I thought the dean's office just wanted to check up on me, to monitor my progress and make sure I was holding up under the stress. Having attended the college for some years before I reenrolled, I knew most of the staff and faculty on a first-name basis.

I sat in John Churchill's office as he delivered one of my least favorite lines: "Roger, this hurts me more than it hurts you."

The decision to expel me, Churchill maintained, had come from the board itself.

The board's decision would have rested better with me if Churchill had possessed character enough to admit he agreed with my expulsion. John said he didn't agree with the action, but that it was beyond his power to reverse. I found this hard to believe. Other members of the faculty who went to bat for me found they had no recourse, but Churchill surely did.

I called Bill at his office in Little Rock.

"I want to stay," I told him, "and let them expel me."

He took a big breath, then let it out in an audible sigh. "I'm tired of fighting it," he told me. "We don't need to worry about these people."

He wanted me to voluntarily withdraw from Hendrix.

As I suspected, money was the driving force behind Churchill's decision. He and the board feared the publicity surrounding my upcoming trial would not sit well with potential donors, and might even cause some Hendrix benefactors to reconsider their decision to give money to the college. The administration, in my case, could not stand behind the student.

I went home and became sick. Someone called Mother and she and her husband Dick came to Little Rock as quickly as they could. When they got there, they saw me looking like death warmed over. I had thrown up everything I tried to eat and could barely stand, feeling pale and weak as I explained to them I had gone to the dean and begged for a chance to stay in school.

There was still another two and a half months to go before my trial. With the stabilizing force of my college life gone, all I could do was sit in Little Rock and wait. However, there was something going on: My brother's campaign for reelection was in its final week.

⇒ ELECTION DAY 1984 ⇐

Tuesday, November 6, was Election Day. Bill's Republican opponent was Woody Freeman. Like Frank White, who defeated Bill in 1980, Freeman told voters across Arkansas he intended to run state government like a business. He pledged not to raise taxes and maintained he would correct what he called "Bill Clinton's mistakes in office." This election, Freeman said, would be a referendum on my brother's entire tenure in office.

The people of Arkansas rallied around my brother, and he handily won the election with 63 percent of the vote. Freeman's 37 percent share came largely from the Republican-dominated northwest corner of Arkansas. I was grateful my arrest had not cost my brother his hard-earned victory.

At the same time, it saddened me that I had not participated in my brother's campaign, although I had participated in every previous Clinton campaign—from his race for Congress in 1974, through the victorious attorney general effort, his first gubernatorial bid, and his comeback campaign in 1982. This time I sat on the sidelines, fearing that any involvement on my part would damage his reelection effort.

Through November and December, I stayed in my apartment in Little Rock. It was close to the Governor's Mansion and my brother often wanted to see me. He took care of me, paying out of his own pocket for transportation, food, and clothes. With my trial only weeks away, I found it hard to find a job. I turned to a friend, a wonderful man named Rocky Willmuth, whose family owned a chain of convenience stores called the General Oil Company. Rocky put me to work in one of his stores during the holiday season. Later, during the trial, Rocky and his father, Paul, testified on my behalf as character witnesses. Rocky and Paul, who has since passed away, will always have a special place in my heart for giving me a chance when no one outside my family would.

I don't remember much about the 1984 Christmas season. As you might expect, it was a joyless time for me. I was thankful I was alive, my family was supporting me, and I was no longer heavily addicted to cocaine. While I still partied on occasion during the months leading to my trial, I never sold the drug again or used any large amount of cocaine personally. I did use small amounts a few times between my arrest and trial.

Most people might wonder how someone facing trial for possession and distribution of cocaine could use the drug again, even rarely. I had observed my birthday, my tenth high school class reunion, Halloween, Thanksgiving, Christmas, and the New Year, laboring under the knowledge I was going to prison. My attitude was belligerent and denied responsibility for my actions. What more could the authorities do? Arrest me? I guess I was still sick, but as it turned out, the first few weeks in prison would break my addiction completely.

On New Year's Eve, 1984, I went to a Little Rock club to greet 1985 in some sort of a festive spirit. Although I had not done drugs for several weeks, I used cocaine that night. It marked one of the final times I indulged, as well as one of my last nights of freedom.

The arrival of the New Year gave me little reason to celebrate, for I was certain to be going to prison in a matter of days. I watched dispassionately as preparations advanced for my brother's inaugural, when he would take the oath of office and begin his third term as governor. One of the phrases from the inaugural address he was writing seemed directed at me.

> We must believe in ourselves and our ability to
> shape our own destiny. Too many of us still expect

too little of ourselves and demand too little of each
other because we see the future as a question of fate,
out of our hands. But the future need not be fate; it
can be an achievement.

Just a few days after the inaugural ceremonies, I went to trial
in Hot Springs. Since I had pled guilty to a pair of charges, the
entire proceedings lasted only a couple of hours. But as brief as
it was, the event was still quite a spectacle.

⟶ ON TRIAL ⟵

The media turned out for the trial in full force. Television cameras and newspaper reporters filled the courtroom, their lenses
focused on my mother, my brother, and me. I pled guilty to one
charge of my choosing; the other was chosen by the government.
I decided to plead guilty to the charge of distribution of a single gram of cocaine—a very small amount, considering that, at
the time of my arrest, I was doing five to seven grams per day.
The federal charge was "conspiracy to distribute," which meant
I knew, discussed, and planned a drug deal. This was the best
charge the government could manage, as they had no evidence—
no drugs, no money.

The judge was a kindly man named Oren Harris, who was
very close to Bill. At the time of my trial, he was nearing eighty
years of age. The man who had fingered my Colombian partner
and me was sentenced to a year in prison. The authorities had
promised not to indict him if he told them the names of others

he knew to be involved in drug trafficking, and I was one of those he named. The day after this man identified me, he was indicted on federal drug charges.

Next to be sentenced was my partner, the young Colombian who had suggested that I flee the country with him. Because he had been in jail since July, he'd built up six months' time already served. The two years he received meant he only had to serve another eighteen months.

Rocky and Paul Willmuth testified on my behalf, and Bill had already talked with Judge Harris privately. It would have been a conflict of interest on Bill's part to testify publicly on my behalf.

"This is a touchy situation," Bill explained to me, adding it wasn't "proper" for a sitting governor to speak for a relative during a court proceeding. I just had to accept that fact.

During the trial, Bill and Mother sat on either side of me, each holding one of my hands. Bill often leaned over to tell me everything would be okay.

"You're going to do your time and then this whole thing will be over with," he said.

Despite the best efforts of the Willmuths and my brother (behind the scenes), I had no doubt I would draw a heavier sentence than the two just handed down by Judge Harris, and the state's entire press contingent was there to see my brother's reaction. What would he do? Would I skate on my sentence? As it turned out, the judge sentenced me to five years; three on the conspiracy to distribute charge, and two years for possession of the single gram of cocaine.

Then, Judge Harris did a wonderful thing. He reduced my prison time to two years, with three years' probation.

"I cannot, in good conscience," he said from the bench, "take away five years of your life." Although Judge Harris's own precedent had shown he was inclined to be more lenient than this, I appreciated the reduction in sentence. While I would be out of prison in twenty-four months, I really had to watch my step for the three years following my release.

I came to the courtroom that day prepared to go to prison. Normally, the courts give you a few days to put your affairs in order, but I didn't see any point in postponing the inevitable. After I was sentenced, I was moved to a back room in the courthouse. I took off my Christian Dior suit, put on a pair of sweats, and was led out of the room in handcuffs by the marshals.

On the way out I was allowed to say good-bye to my mother and brother, the people who mattered most to me. Court officials brought Bill and Mother around to the back after letting the crowd file out and gave us fifteen minutes with each other. There wasn't a whole lot to say, but the three of us put our arms around each other in a little circle and cried and cried. It was a sad time, but a turning point for us as well. We had agreed this was a bottoming-out time for me and that my life was already back on the rebound. There was nothing negative about that.

My mind had begun to clear, and I was thinking better. I realized I was tired of running. It was time I gave my brother back his brother and my mother her younger son. We even laughed nervously a little bit, talking about how I was putting my life back together. It was an attempt to add some levity to the situation.

During those last few moments together, Bill admonished me to take responsibility for myself: "We will get through this and we are here for you, but you have to show us *you* want to get better."

He sounded confident and positive, giving me one of those reassuring smiles of his. He was probably trying to reassure himself a little bit, too. I knew I *was* getting better—I was honestly on my way back up.

But positive words, suggestions, encouragement, and pep talks only work so well. I still had lots of soul-searching and growing up to do. For better or worse, I would do it in prison.

BOUND FOR PRISON

We were bound for Texarkana, Arkansas—a border town that extends into Texas. My former partner and I were handcuffed together in the back seat of a government vehicle, with two federal marshals sitting in front. As we drove down the wooded, winding road south of Hot Springs, I looked out at Lake DeGray, knowing I wouldn't be seeing the lake again for a long time. Dusk was approaching as we left the heavily populated areas behind, heading southwest for Interstate 30 through the pine forests towards the state line.

The highway meets the interstate near the city of Arkadelphia, a small college town situated roughly midway between Little Rock and Texarkana. As we approached the interstate entrance ramp, I asked the marshal if we could stop at the McDonald's that was, of course, conveniently located near the ramp. Obligingly, he drove beneath the overpass and into the McDonald's, then paid for the cheeseburger I ordered. Since I had no money with me, it was a kind thing for him to do. I wanted to taste just one last cheeseburger before I went to prison, although I don't remember it tasting especially good. It was just a vestige of my former life I could latch onto and remember during the days that lay ahead. As you may have heard, a weakness for fast-food runs in the family.

For a brief moment, I thought of trying to escape while we were stopped in Arkadelphia—a reflexive moment of leftover foolishness.

Darkness had long since fallen when we neared Texarkana. We rolled into the federal correctional facility in absolute silence, and the guards shut the large gates behind us. As I was led from the car and into the prisoner reception area, I felt frightened, ashamed, and totally alone. The prison officials took all my belongings—which consisted of my contact lenses and their case—and threw me a T-shirt, khaki pants, and some cloth shoes. The shoes did not fit and they didn't even match each other. "Get used to it," one of the jailers told me.

You see jail scenes in movies where guards march prisoners down a long corridor, shove the unhappy inmate into a small cell, and slam the barred door shut. Well, that's the way it really is.

The cell itself wasn't exactly spacious—it measured about six feet by nine feet with a bed bolted to the floor along one side. There was a stationary cot, sink, toilet, radiator, heater, and a barred window about seven or eight feet off the ground. The walls on the right, left, and at the back were solid, not made of steel bars. There was no room for a cellmate, and I couldn't see into the cells alongside. I could see only the cell directly across the hall from mine, and the cells diagonally across.

One of the first tricks I learned during my time behind bars was to use a shard from a mirror to see the inmates in the cells next to me. Prisoners would break mirrors on purpose, then pass out the pieces. Depending on your inmate status or seniority, you might get a tiny bit of mirror or a larger piece. It was the only social contact we could manage.

Someone—either inmates or the prison officials—had clipped accounts of my upcoming sentencing from that morning's Little Rock newspapers. Now, as I walked past the cells on my block, I could see the articles festooned on cell walls like Christmas decorations. I guess everyone in the facility wanted to make sure I "felt at home" from the very first night.

I took a few moments to survey my small domain. There was barely enough room on the floor to do sit-ups and push-ups, although the cell was relatively clean—very clean compared to some of the later facilities where I spent time. The federal maximum-security facility in El Reno, Oklahoma, was so filthy I couldn't believe people survived there.

I collapsed on the cot, crying and scared. The only thing I wanted to do now was talk to God. Even though I had reached a point in my life where few people believed me anymore, I knew that wasn't the case with God.

As best as I can recall, my prayer that first night was this:

> God, You know I'm not a religious person.
> When I was little, I couldn't understand certain
> things regarding death and my family, and You
> never did seem to explain them to me. But I'm
> coming to You now to tell You from my heart, I
> can't make it if You don't help me.

I hoped God was keeping up with me, because this conversation was about to go somewhere:

> I don't think I'm strong enough to make it
> on my own. If I do make it, I'll know You were with
> me. I'm a spiritual person, and You know good and
> well, God, I'm not going to be carrying a Bible
> around in prison for appearance's sake, no matter
> how long I'm here. I'm not going to be preaching
> the word simply to lessen my time. So it's up to You
> whether I make it or not. My mother and my
> brother aren't here, and I need someone who loves
> me unconditionally. If You don't help me, I won't
> make it.

God also knew He could see right through me. I had really turned my back on God, although I must have believed in Him because I was cussing Him so much. I told Him:

> Here I am again, God. If You think of me
> as a good person, or You get so doggone mad at

me You just want to spit, I've always believed You had a good enough sense of humor to deal with people like me on earth. The bottom line is, You know who I am, and if I'm worth saving, You'll give me the strength. If I make it, that'll be my answer. All these years, I've always wanted answers. When I was a little boy, I wanted to know why my dad beat me, my mother, and my brother. Then I wondered why You didn't take my abusive dad away from us.

As I thought back on that, praying as hard as I could in my prison cell, I had been praying for God to take my dad away because I was afraid of him. At the time I didn't understand alcoholism and sicknesses and I just thought he was a mean, bad person. As young as I was, I couldn't understand why God made him like that.

Then, after he died, I wanted to know why I didn't have a dad. I never could get any immediate answers, so I began alienating myself from the church, telling God I didn't like what He had done. If He was so good—as I had learned in Sunday school—why was He letting so many bad things happen to my family?

I grew away from the church, although I never grew away from my spirituality—my personal relationship with God. I did not practice it as well as I should have, but I was aware of it. When I went back to church later in life, I was disgusted to hear of all these different denominations and factions each claiming to be the true disciples and worshipers of God. These were people who "knew" or "were in touch with" God, yet were arguing with each other. They claimed to be deeply religious, yet they couldn't agree on anything.

I still go to church from time to time, but that kind of denominational fighting made me realize I had to depend on a personal relationship with God. I've always been a true believer, whether it meant I was thankful for what He did or angry at Him. My first conversation with God in prison was difficult for me, but it helped. A few nights later, I started recording my thoughts on scrap paper, and a portion of the journal I kept during my months in prison is reproduced later in this book.

A fellow inmate from Stuttgart, Arkansas—a guy we called "Hoghead"—loaned me a bit of scrap paper and a pencil. But that first night, I don't know if I could have written anything down; I was too overwhelmed. The days that stretched before me were too many to comprehend, and just making it through the night seemed beyond me. I came close to crying myself to sleep, but at some time during the evening, the tears stopped. God was answering my prayer, and I began to see through the fear that enveloped me. He was with me that night, I'm certain.

My final thought as the darkness of sleep overtook me was: With the help of God, and with the love of my family and friends, I can make it out of here.

CHAPTER FOUR

JAILHOUSE JOURNAL

When I began my jailhouse journal, I did not know how important it would become in my life. At times, it was my only certain comfort. I would go to it to broadcast my fears, gripes, discomforts, and frustrations. I would note the importance of my family's support, discussions with my new-found friends, and the few joys allotted me in jail.

I keep it as a reminder that there are always consequences for every action, and I should weigh those consequences more carefully than I did in the past.

I share it so that others will know what took me so long to understand: That sometimes those who love you the most must make you face those consequences to learn, and that does not mean they are abandoning you.

THE BEGINNING
Monday, January 27, 1985

I arrived in Texarkana at 7:00 P.M. to begin serving my two-year sentence and was held in "segregated confinement," which is somewhat misleading because there are blacks, Mexicans, Indians, and other minorities on my floor. The man to my immediate right has been here forty-four months for four armed bank robberies. The black man across the hall "was standing next to a man when a wall just happened to fall on his head and crush it."

I really fit in here, don't I? I was issued clothes (khaki), dirty and mismatched, dirty linen, and a one-man cell that measures six feet by ten feet—home for at least a week. The head crusher, "Flip," seems all right; so do the other two: "Weird," the bank robber, and "Hoghead," the guy who lent me this pen and paper. He's from Stuttgart, Arkansas. "Weird" and "Hoghead" *bark* a lot. Usually at any of the officers, or at each other, but sometimes for no apparent reason. Oh well, I guess I'll be all right as long as I don't start *barking!*

My bed is stationary and the ceiling leaks directly over it, so I hope it doesn't rain before I leave. I was issued *green* Peter Pan slippers—size nine although I wear ten and a half. Lights out is at 10:30. I must keep praying and hoping I will make it through tonight and tomorrow. I love my family, my friends, and my life. Forever.

DAY 5

Friday, February 1, 1985

A new month that I hope will fly by. We got two inches of snow last night, and it is still coming down this morning. Another four to five inches are expected today, so the prospects of leaving for Fort Worth are not looking too good. As long as I can get there by February 6, because I think that's the day my brother narrates the nationally televised program in response to Reagan's speech— I'm not allowed to see it here. The three meals were bad today, starting with breakfast. I wasn't quite awake, I guess, and what I thought was oatmeal got my immediate attention. I used my only sugar on it rather than on my cornflakes, and buttered it up and then took my first bite—it was cream gravy. There was nothing to do but laugh, set my tray down and go back to sleep. Lunch was no better, although Mary Schroeder came after lunch, and I got forty-five minutes to visit with her. It was great! I let out a little bitterness that's been inside me since my sentencing, but overall I'm in a good frame of mind.

DAY 6
Saturday, February 2, 1985

I received a wonderful surprise visit today from my mother and stepfather, Dick, who drove from Hot Springs to see me. I was so happy to see them, I cried. They're spending the night in Texarkana so they can spend all day here tomorrow (8:30 A.M.—3:00 P.M.). I hope I can get some sleep tonight, because in addition to the excitement and the anticipation of tomorrow's visit, the ceiling over my bed has begun to leak. That's okay, I'll just sleep on the floor—I've certainly done that once or twice in my lifetime.

I exercise quite a bit everyday; it's almost time for my next session of push-ups, sit-ups, leg lifts, and side-straddle hops. I think I'm getting stronger every day—mentally, emotionally, physically, and *even spiritually*. Will wonders never cease?

DAY 7—Final day in Texarkana
Sunday, February 3, 1985

I woke up around 5:00 A.M. too excited to sleep any longer, but I did sleep well during the night. Coffee cake was served around

6:00 A.M., then I lay back down for a little while and watched the sunrise. It was nothing spectacular, but the clouds did clear off about 8:30 A.M., leaving a beautiful blue sky. Mother and Dick arrived around 9:00 A.M., and we visited all day till 3:15 P.M. It was such a wonderful day—I really can't explain my feelings inside today. That's not all to be excited about—today was my last day in Texarkana—I can't believe it. I'm Fort Worth-bound via El Reno (Oklahoma City) and Seagoville (Dallas). The trip will take fifteen hours and an overnight to get me to a destination three hours away.

DAY 8
Monday, February 4, 1985
We made an early start today at 4:00 A.M. although our actual departure for El Reno, outside of Oklahoma City, was delayed until about 6:30 A.M. due to federal red tape. We arrived in El Reno about 3:00 P.M. were relieved of the chains and cuffs we had worn the entire trip, and were then processed into that facility. We were issued different clothes (a bright red jumpsuit, which is more to my taste than the khakis), our pictures were taken again, and three hours later we got a bologna sandwich for dinner and were taken to where we were staying. I did get lucky as I was the only one that got to stay in the camp while everyone else had to stay in the tiny double holding cells. My camp had no fence around it and was equipped with pool tables, table tennis, and weights. I felt a little guilty for getting so lucky, and I wondered about the other prisoners' reactions, but the next morning everything was fine.

Before falling asleep, I lay awake in the bed wondering about what the Fort Worth facility will be like. I hope everything is better from here on because I'm trying so hard. I still get down and aggravated at times, but I know everyone's still behind me, including God.

DAY 9
Tuesday, February 5, 1985

Another early start—we woke at 3:30 A.M. and were dressed and at the breakfast table by 3:50 A.M. We are on our way to Fort Worth, finally, but make a stop in Seagoville (Dallas) and a van takes me to Fort Worth from there, about a forty-five mile drive. When we get off the bus in Seagoville, they take the cuffs and chains off the six of us for a thirty-foot walk to the van going to Fort Worth, then the marshals replace the cuffs and chains. We arrive around 12:30 P.M. and started getting reprocessed into Fort Worth—another strip search, pictures taken again, more papers to sign, the same ones I've already signed. I finally receive the one change of clothes that I wore from court. The good thing is that we are walking around and being treated like humans—the cuffs and chains are gone. Some necessities—shampoo, razor, etc.—are loaned to me, and the guard gives me soap, blades for the loaned razor, and a toothbrush but no toothpaste. I'm issued linen and a blanket, but no mattress, or a locker. I finally get those two around 10:00 P.M. I'm almost set, and I'm about to drop from exhaustion. Room count is at 10:30 P.M. and another at midnight, 2:30 A.M., and 4:30 A.M. I'm sure I'm not leaving! I played a little pool tonight, met a few people, and watched the prison team play a basketball game.

DAY 10
Wednesday, February 6, 1985

I awoke around 6:00 A.M., walked over to breakfast which consisted of four eggs, toast with jelly, and cereal, which I didn't have time to eat, and then went to my dental, lab, and clinic appointments—everything was fine. My counselor, Mary Howard, visited with me. She sort of "pre-oriented" me concerning some of the most important aspects here: mail, visitation, and the programs offered. I found out which nights I'll be attending Narcotics Anonymous (Tuesday 7:00-8:00 P.M.) and Alcoholics Anonymous (Wednesday 7:30-8:30 P.M.), so I'm fairly well prepared going into tomorrow's orientation. My group starts at 7:55 A.M., so after tomorrow I should be a little more familiar with my surroundings. Jay M. (Baton Rouge), Vic A. (Kansas City), John H. (Dallas), and Fred B. (Holden, Mo.) have really been great since I got here. They've either loaned me or rounded up anything I've needed. It's tough not having anything of your own other than one change of clothes. Mother to the rescue. My box of everything should be here in a week.

This is a co-ed facility and the women are becoming more and more "friendly," although I've only been here two days. I am trying not to think about them. I had a good run and workout today, then went to the recreational room and played pool and Ping-Pong. Everyone else has the flu, but I feel healthy and all in all it was another good day. It's time for bed, but first my contacts, then a prayer to thank God for helping me through one more day.

DAY 11
Thursday, February 7, 1985

The word is going around that I've been placed here as a "snitch." I'm going to try and ignore this because of its absurdity. Fortunately, some of my fellow inmates don't seem susceptible to this ridiculous rumor. This, too, shall pass.

I like writing at night but I better wrap it up for now. Thank God, one more behind me. I love my family, my friends, and my life forever.

DAY 12
Friday, February 8, 1985

Today I went to my orientation group and watched a film on certain procedures here. Then, I signed up for an appointment with the psychologist to let him know I wasn't crazy all the time. Ha!

Mail call was right before supper and I got five letters from friends and family: from Mary Jane, Lynda Dixon, Dr. Haggard, David Brown, and Mother (a culmination of five letters in one). I miss M. J. and David a lot because I've been so close to them for so long. I sure hope Larry and M. J. have a great year at Oaklawn and an even better one next year! I filled out my visitation list and will turn it in tomorrow. The people on the list have to return a questionnaire to the facility before they can be allowed to see me. If they are sent promptly maybe I can have my first visitors by next weekend. I hope to see my girlfriend Shawn *soon*—I love her. She's so wonderful! I didn't work out tonight, just watched television instead, but on the productive side I did wash the few clothes I have, having finally received some detergent from the unit officer.

DAY 13
Saturday, February 9, 1985

I was finishing a letter when one Lee J., a sixty-five-year-old black man from Arkansas who looks quite a bit older than his years, interrupted me. He wanted to talk a little politics which led to a general discussion of domestic and world problems. I've gotten to be pretty good friends with Lee since I've been here, and he's a really interesting guy. Something he said stuck with me (by the way, he has only completed school through the third grade): "Roger, the country will ultimately and only be pulled together by a black man. Martin Luther King, Jr., was the beginning. People don't like things changing that they are accustomed to; so won't the whites [sic]. We might not see it in our lifetime—oh, you might—for we have so far to go and such a short time to get there. Remember what Khrushchev believed: 'Russia doesn't have to worry, because the U.S. will destroy itself,' and I believe that, unless we are saved by a black man." He has a really thoughtful perspective, and who knows, years from now....

DAY 14
Sunday, February 10, 1985

I'm a bit confused about this place, because there just doesn't seem to be as elaborate a rehabilitation program as I had expected. It might, however, start living up to its reputation this week as I close out my tedious orientation period. I hope so. Excuse me for thinking about something here that I probably shouldn't waste time on, but there is such an incredible amount of financial waste in the federal prison system, or at least the ones I've seen so far. Someone should be placed in the prisons to review how the federal money is spent or rather misspent and to find out where the budget could and should be trimmed (many places and areas). Listen to me, I sound like *Roger Nader!*

DAY 17
Wednesday, February 13, 1985

Today I put on the only piece of jewelry I have here, and I'm not going to take it off. It's my good-luck charm and always has been. It's a St. Jude Thaddeus medal—he is the patron saint of the impossible, and it was given to me by a very special friend from Hot Springs—Arnold Doubleday.

DAY 18—Valentine's Day
Thursday, February 14, 1985

I didn't get much sleep last night but got up around 7:00 A.M. to take the required SAT test at 7:45 A.M., my final step in the orientation program. I tried to call Mother and wish her a happy

Valentine's Day, but she was already gone to town, I guess. I'm a bit lonely on my first holiday in prison, and it didn't help by missing Mother at home. Shawn's phone is still screened from collect calls, so I couldn't reach her today either. I went to lunch feeling a bit down, but in the cafeteria line I met a girl named Debbie from Washington, D.C. She has pretty eyes and an even prettier smile. Maybe I can find out her last name tomorrow. Anyway, before we got our food, she got my attention and said, "Roger, happy Valentine's Day." As strange as this may sound, I think this particular Valentine's greeting was more special than any other in my lifetime.

Today I was given a job assignment and rather than being placed in the kitchen like most new inmates, I was named an orderly of my unit (Star). There are 211 people in my unit and only eight orderlies, so I was fortunate to get this job which requires only that I work about three or four hours in the A.M. The rest of the day, I can do whatever I want, within limits, which will allow me to keep up my correspondence and to work out in the afternoon rather than early in the morning. Maybe someone is looking down on me. I also found out my mom and stepdad are coming to visit this weekend, and *I can't wait!* I hope my brother, sister-in-law, and niece will visit soon as well.

DAY 19
Friday, February 15, 1985
My first day of work coincided with an inspection day, so the unit had to be as immaculate as possible. Starting around 8:00 A.M.,

I swept, dusted, mopped, and got the trash together. I had to stop around 10:30 A.M. so I could make my 10:50 A.M. doctor's appointment for my left knee and my hands. Lunch was next followed by a meeting of the Tarrant County Alcohol and Drug Abuse program which began at 1:00 P.M. and would last until 4:00 P.M., but I had to leave at 3:00 P.M. to pick up my pills and medicated hand cream.

I'm feeling better every day now. It's strange how meeting Debbie has made me feel more upbeat. I don't know if it's because of needed companionship, or what, but I like it. I'm going to find out more about her tomorrow, like maybe her last name. Not being able to call Shawn for two weeks now hasn't helped matters anyway. Her phone could definitely have been de-screened by now. I tell myself not to worry about the outside world, because I'm not a part of it now. I just want to serve my time, concentrate on reality, and keep the faith! My first visit happens tomorrow, and I hope everything goes smoothly, as far as the red tape goes. I'm going to tell Mother and Dick about everything I'm involved in here: programs, activities and people...I don't know if I'll tell them that Debbie is here on a murder charge (thirty-five years). Now I've got to get some rest. I'm coming to talk to you, Lord. Thank you for one more good one.

DAY 20
Saturday, February 16, 1985
Mother and Dick looked great, and the day couldn't have been more beautiful. The temperature was close to sixty degrees with a

stiff breeze out of the southwest and a cloudless blue sky. We
talked about everything: my NA and AA programs, the sports
activities available, things I still need, people and events here and
back home, the races, and any and every other thing that popped
in our heads. It was great! What's even better is that they are coming again tomorrow from about 11:00 A.M. to 3:00 P.M. My
church service ends at 11:00 A.M., and I'll go straight over after
that. I'm certain we'll have plenty to talk about; especially about
Debbie H. from Fairfax, Virginia, and Washington, D.C. I finally
found out her last name. I told her it would be really nice to know
a little more about her than just Debbie...she agreed! After the
visit, she and I went to eat supper, a light one, then went to the
track and walked around several times just visiting, sharing opinions, thoughts, and feelings. I thank you, Lord. I will make it, I
know it—God willing. I love my family.

DAY 22
Monday, February 18, 1985

Happy birthday, George Washington. What is your honest opinion on how your son, our country, is doing? That's what I was
afraid you would say. It was another good day "down under," one
more to cross off that calendar I don't have. I'll get one this week
along with a watch and an alarm clock. I also have to get some
twenty-two-cent stamps. At the rate of recent postal increases, I'm
sure I'll live to see the price of a stamp rival the price of a gallon
of gas; but that is the least of my worries, which, by the way, are
rapidly diminishing.

I saw Debbie again today. She was a bit upset today, due to an altercation with another girl here. But knowing Debbie, I have no doubt that she can handle herself, regardless of the solution she implements. I think she comes from a mixed race background; I'd like to know more about her. I find her really interesting. I love my family, my friends, and my life, forever! Thank you, Lord. Goodnight.

DAY 23
Tuesday, February 19, 1985

Mail call, at 4:15 P.M., was amazing, again. I got sixteen letters! The mail is the main thing that has kept me going throughout this ordeal. After mail call, however, I was told that I was leaving tomorrow, which depressed me for several reasons. I went outside to try and exercise and ran into Debbie in "the yard." She ran five miles while I played basketball and racquetball. I'm going to miss her a lot—I hope I return here as I'm supposed to. However, I've learned to not assume anything. Debbie and I were going to a dance this weekend, which is a rather rare event here, and that was going to be the first time we could get close physically. Needless to say, we were looking forward to that. Oh well...just another disappointment. My return here will override that disappointment! She's really special, can you tell?

DAY 40
Friday, March 8, 1985

Well, today is March 8, and on this day every year I think about one particular thing—Karen Marie Meyers' birthday. She would have been twenty-nine years old today had she not drowned almost ten years ago. It was such a tragedy. She was my first real girlfriend, and she was a beautiful fifteen-year-old. The sad thing is that I've lost contact with her family and I don't know how to reach them to reestablish contact. Happy Birthday, Karen. (Speaking of B-Days, Debbie's is on March 22, so it's right around the corner). I finally came out about 8:15 P.M. to get my medicine (Motrin) for my leg, as the pill line opens at 9:00 P.M. for half an hour. Debbie hadn't been out all day because she was depressed by something personal, but she came out to the pill line and we talked after getting our medicine. She was really down, but it's understandable.

DAY 41
Saturday, March 9, 1985

At 4:00 P.M., I got the visit I've been waiting for—Bill. We talked about the legislative session which is just drawing to a close. He's concerned about a gasoline tax bill that he didn't propose, but it looks as if it will be adopted and he must decide whether to veto the bill or not. If he does, he might lose some support from some of the legislators who support his education bills. If he does not veto the bill, he might lose a considerable percentage of support from the Arkansas electorate. It's a tough decision, but I know his primary concern lies with the education bills. We also talked about my routine here, my attitude, the people and administration, Debbie and her situation, Dan and George, and other things going on back home. It was so good seeing him. After he left, I returned to the unit and then went to the yard to meet Debbie.

We sat and talked until 8:00 P.M., and then went to a "concert" in the gym performed by a young, three-piece rock band that needed a lot of practice. Everyone started leaving after about twenty minutes, but we stuck it out for forty-five, mainly out of respect for their efforts. Then we went to the pill line before coming in for the evening. I started reading the book that Dan sent me, *Roosevelt As We Knew Him*. It seems as if it's going to be very interesting, and maybe this beginning will be the kick I've needed to increase my desire to read.

DAY 42
March 10, 1985

I went out to the yard after 4:00 P.M. count to meet Debbie. I couldn't play racquetball because of my leg, so I lifted weights while she played. We were invited to two different guacamole parties tonight, and after leaving the yard it was time to go to the first one. It lasted until about 6:30 or 7:00 P.M. and we were both in a great mood. I went in to put some long pants on because it was a bit chilly and was to meet Debbie at the other party in about twenty minutes. We'd been at the second party about ten minutes when she decided she was too cold, too tired, and too upset to stay out. A new roommate was moving in with her which she did not like for several reasons. I walked her back in, but a few minutes later she came back out and didn't even speak to me the rest of the night. Too tired, too cold, too upset to be outside with me.

Around 9:00 P.M., I walked right up to her, but she refused to acknowledge my presence. She then walked with another guy for over an hour before he walked her back to her unit, directly under my window. She says I'm naive, but I'm not that naive. I just don't like being fooled with or taken for granted.

DAY 43
March 11, 1985

Today, day 43, I thought often of Shawn. Forty-three was a significant number while we lived together. This day also marked the end of my close relationship with Debbie H. She became very negative this past week about me, other inmates, and officers, and I can't figure her out because she had no reason to treat me like this. Roger, welcome to the world of prison relationships! Goodbye Debbie, and good luck. You'll need it! I wish you happiness and strength!

Enter Vicki from Sweetwater, Texas. She is a very attractive, blond, blue-eyed, well-built twenty-four-year-old bank manager-turned-embezzler. What a wonderful girl to come into my life at this crucial time. Oh well, here I go again.

DAY 46
March 14, 1985

Vicki and I passed up dinner and met out in the yard between 5:15 and 5:30 P.M. My stress management class started at 6:00 P.M., so after a few minutes together, she walked me over to the group. I met her out front at 7:00 P.M. and we went to a wonderful church service in the chapel from 7:30 to 9:00 P.M. I'm going to make this Thursday night service as often as possible. The congregation is 75 percent black, and it is an energetic and lively service. Very uplifting, spiritually—it made my day. And naturally, I love it more because of the music and type of singing. There is so much soul and feeling in the music—right up my alley! Vicki talked me into going, so I owe her one. Afterwards, she and I went to the rec room and visited awhile, then I walked her to her unit at 9:45 P.M. Returned to my room to write this under my new, battery-operated lamp that Mother sent me. She thinks of everything—even prison underwear (black-and-white striped). What a sense of humor she has! I love her so much.

DAY 47
March 15, 1985

I'm getting stronger, working out every day, usually after the 4:00 P.M. count. After my workout today, Vicki came out in the yard to meet me and we walked until about 6:15 P.M., before going to the chapel. I was to meet Bob Campbell, the church organist, who also cuts and styles hair here on the compound. He wanted me to come and sing while he played some different songs. I'm going to start singing in and out of church, and Bob is interested in getting an entertainment program started, religious or not. Anyway, he had forgotten about a previous program already scheduled to meet in the chapel, so we called it off until after brunch tomorrow. Vicki and I stayed in the lobby outside the chapel for another hour or so, talking, and then around 8:00 P.M. she had to go to the visiting room—her husband had come to see her. That situation was quite strange, needless to say, since it was my first experience of that nature.

DAY 53
March 21, 1985

I haven't felt compelled to write for the past few days. My lapse wasn't due to the fact that I was depressed, rather, I was tired a lot earlier than usual. I've been hitting the proverbial sack around 10:00 or 11:00 P.M., since I meet Vicki for breakfast every morning at 6:30 A.M. It's been an interesting past couple of days, and very enjoyable. I've spent most of my free time with and around Vicki. If I'm playing tennis or softball, she usually comes to watch and we eat breakfast and lunch together, skip dinner, and spend the rest of the evening together. She's really very pretty, sweet, and funny. She was telling me about breaking in her room, and we decided it was appropriate to do that here. This resolution brought about a prison proverb: While free, it's better to break out than break in, but while in prison, it's better to break in than break out. I'm a little shaken up because our relationship seems to be growing every day. I don't exactly know what to think about it, although I realize that I'm starting to care for her a lot. Remember, however, she's married, and is also having marital problems. I feel that I'm alleviating the problems, rather than unconsciously or unintentionally causing them, at least, I hope that's the case. Regardless, I care for her a great deal—she's special.

DAY 87
April 24, 1985

Well, it's been a month and I'm finally back in the mood to start writing again. I ended all communication with Shawn and took her off my visitation list, mainly because after a full month she still hadn't taken the time to fill out the simple questionnaire and return it, a prerequisite to visitation. That really disturbed me because I have loved her for a long time, and we went through so much together. I tried not to think about her and to focus on other things, like talking to Chelsea, knowing Mother was coming to visit this Saturday, and having a special person from my recent past—Maren Cook—inform me she wants to come visit in a couple of weeks. A few days ago, April 21, was the anniversary of my car wreck, which gave me a special opportunity to give thanks to God for allowing me to be alive. There is a specific reason, and I'm getting closer to realizing what God's plan is for me. That's the main thing that keeps me going.

DAY 100
May 7, 1985

I don't know why, but I'm treating this day with some significance, due to it being my hundredth day down. The weeks seem to go by so quickly, but the days crawl. I still feel as if I'm so far from getting out of here. My lawyers (Bill and Steve) have filed my Rule 35 for a sentence reduction and I'm awaiting a response from the judge. I've done everything required here, so I'm hoping Judge Harris will grant the reduction.

Mother and Dick came to visit this past weekend and it was wonderful. I hope to see Bill, Hillary, and Chelsea soon. Bill and Hillary just sent letters, as did cousins Roy, Theresa, and Marie. Thank God my family is still with me.

DAY 137
June 3, 1985

I woke at 7:00 A.M. and had to prepare for a hearing with the Parole Board at 8:15 A.M. The panel decided to give me my minimum guidelines to serve—fourteen months. I could have gotten anywhere from fourteen to twenty months, so I was pretty happy. I'm working on my fifth month. I'll have only five more months to serve here if I am allowed to go to a halfway house for the last four months. If all goes well, I should leave here and return to Arkansas either in November or December, so I'll be home for Christmas.

There was another interesting development today. Helen Allen, a very pretty guard or "hack" as they are called, and I have gotten to be pretty close (not that close!). Anyway, she sent a message for me to come visit her in her new office; she's now manager of the new deli that was built next to the mess hall, so I did, and she said to come back Thursday after dinner to visit. Plus, one of the letters I received today was from Lana Coffman, a jailer in Arkansas at the Pope County Jail. What is the sudden attraction to policewomen? Is it the mystery, the intrigue... I doubt it! Perhaps it's the time I've spent down, and it's just now starting to take effect.

The musical program scheduled for June 18th—"Give My Regards to Broadway"—is coming along just fine. I'm still upset that Mother, Dick, Brother, and family can't come, but I understand the warden's position. Rehearsal tomorrow should be quite intense. I'm spending time these days with Debi D., a pretty Cajun— from uh, oh, my weak spot, New Orleans—I love my family, my friends, and my life forever. Thank you, Lord, goodnight!

DAY 132
June 8, 1985
At the sound of the tone it will be midnight and I'm drinking my late-night Pepsi before retiring for the evening. Earlier when I tried to get a Pepsi, the machine took my money. There is absolutely "no such thing as a free lunch," especially in prison! But not even that could dampen my excitement, which is due to the fact that Bill, Hillary, and Chelsea are coming to visit me tomorrow, and it will be the first time I've seen Hillary and Chelsea. I'll be emotional, I'm sure, to see Chels. They're coming sometime after noon, so I want to get my workout going early. I miss my brother so much, and I'm glad Hillary arranged her plans so she could come see me before she leaves for England later in the afternoon.

Judge Harris decided against any action whatsoever regarding my Rule 35, but he said he would review it again on October 1. I kind of expected that outcome and I'm hoping for good news in October. Regardless, I will make it! Ding (the midnight tone).

DAY 133

June 9, 1985

Well, for some reason I'm in the mood to write again, rather than delay between journal entries, so here it is. The latest addition to my collection of "Prison Proverbs" is a formula—the answer to the proverbial question "Where is the justice?"

The Verdict + The Sentence = The Justice

Sad, but true. Nevertheless, I'm here until October, November, or December, and I will use my time wisely to think, plan, and concentrate on my future, starting immediately upon my release. I am going to be a star! I'm good onstage, in front of people, entertaining them. Music and singing have been such a huge part of my life, the happiest part, and that is exactly what will make my future happy. Here I come world, get ready! Lord, please be with me on this. It's so important!

It was a beautiful day today. I exercised for about an hour on weights, after lunch, and then went for my visit with my brother and sister-in-law. We had a good talk about channeling my energy in one positive direction and guarding against dissipating it. They encouraged me to move somewhere conducive to my career, such as New York, Nashville, or California, and to pursue my dreams 100 percent with everything I have. "They are absolutely right, they've been right all along; they're absolutely right and I was wrong" (Five Man Electrical Band). I was disappointed that Chelsea didn't come with them, but there must have been a good reason. I hated to see them leave today, but that's life. I know they are as proud as I am about what I've accomplished, and we are all so very thankful, thankful to you, Lord, because "I'm alive and feelin' fine" (Five Man Electrical Band). I love my family, my friends, and my life, forever. Goodnight!

DAY 143
June 19, 1985

It is almost bedtime and I'm totally exhausted, but this is a significant entry both because it's the day before the show and because it's Day 143. That number 143 has been a special, mysterious number for me the past couple of years, and also for Shawn. It showed up everywhere, and the irony of today is that I received a letter from Mother with pictures of Shawn that Mother had taken a few weeks ago. Anyway, Shawn and I aren't writing or corresponding, but I've been thinking of her all day today and looking at a picture of her I have up on my bulletin board. I love her so much still, but we've hurt each other enough.

Well, it's showtime in a matter of hours, and other than the assistant warden changing horses in midstream about a few things, everything is ready for the performance. I'm so excited. Our final rehearsal was tonight and the performance was polished. I feel that this program, "Give My Regards to Broadway," is going to be special because we've worked so hard. It's time to sleep—I still have to work in the morning, even on show day. Thank you, God, for this chance tomorrow. Please be listening to me from "Somewhere Over the Rainbow."

DAY 144

June 20, 1985

I'm sitting here, still in my white tails with a pink bow tie and a pink cummerbund, relishing this quiet time of the evening and the feeling of being dressed up. I had almost forgotten how nice it feels to wear a tux or tails. My "return to the stage" was a huge success. The entire production was near perfect, thanks completely to Robert J. (Bob) Campbell. He is a master at what he does (so many things) which in this case was directing, producing, arranging, writing, playing, performing, and choreographing. He was incredible, and is now leaving for a much-deserved furlough.

DAY 158

July 4, 1985

Happy Independence Day—don't fire all your crackers at once!

I came in and called home today, trying to reach Big Brother. He's back from his vacation and I've been unable to talk to him since the musical. I finally reached him at Mimi Irwin's house on Lake Hamilton in Hot Springs, where many of our friends gather annually for a fireworks display. Everyone else I had tried to contact was also there—Mother and Dick, and Nancy and Carme'. That lifted my spirits more, especially hearing that Nancy and Carme' are coming to visit me Monday evening.

Mother told me, after I inquired about his condition, that she had to have King put to sleep yesterday. He had been struck by paralysis due to old age, and his condition rapidly worsened. She had warned me this past weekend that he was doing badly, but I was hoping to get out before any drastic measures were taken. I really loved King and he was the last thing my stepfather, Jeff, gave me before he died. Nevertheless, he lived to the ripe, old age of twelve years (that's eighty-four), and I guess it was time for him to move on. Mother saw him suffering and did what she thought best.

I do have some great pictures and some wonderful memories of King, just as I do of Jeff, and I guess that's the most anyone can ask for.

DAY 179
July 25, 1985

Happy Birthday, Rog. I just thought I would stay up to wish myself a happy twenty-ninth. I've put in for my furlough August 17 through 20 and am anxiously awaiting confirmation. If I am granted the leave, it means I'll get to be home for Bill's birthday. This place is starting to bother me, and I need a few days away. The only thing that keeps me happy is Debi D. I helped her in the kitchen today washing dishes, just so we could be together a little more time out of the day. I've developed a special love for this young lady and the feeling is mutual. She's sweet, funny, pretty, thoughtful, provocative, and, above all, intelligent. You can't believe how much it means that she's intelligent. The majority of people here have a very limited educational background and some have virtually none at all, which is very sad.

DAY 191

August 6, 1985

The end to another beautiful day is upon me. We are having a typically hot Texas summer and today was the tenth or eleventh consecutive day that the temperature has exceeded one hundred degrees. At least the humidity here is considerably less than in Arkansas. An unexpected benefit of the heat is that one can really lose weight quickly. I've lost a total of forty pounds so far, and I think I will try to maintain this weight now. Being so slim makes me feel twenty years old again.

My furlough has been provisionally approved, but applies only in the Dallas-Fort Worth area. That will still be a blessing, just so I can leave here and "be free" for a few days, but I really was counting on seeing my family and being home for my brother's birthday. Oh well, I'll make the best of it, regardless of the final decision.

I'm despondent and irritable because Debi D. is going home to New Orleans on Friday morning at 8:00 A.M., hopefully for good. I'm glad she's getting out of this place so she can begin her new life, but she's made me so happy during the past three months that I hate to see her go.

DAY 224

September 8, 1985

Yesterday was Special Olympics day here at the prison. We put on a softball tournament and four schools from the Dallas-Fort Worth area sent teams to participate. Booths with games

We named our band "Dealer's Choice" after a pinball machine.

Here I am in my element, performing outdoors with the other members of the band.

Heading into the courthouse in Hot Springs with my attorneys. Within a couple of hours, I'd be on my way to prison.

Mother was there to meet me the day I was released. We celebrated on the prison steps.

Singing at Ricky Frazier's wedding. I'd been out of prison for about eighteen months.

Batter up! This was a benefit softball game in which Mother and I participated. We raised money for disabled horse jockeys.

With Jan Hooks and Meshach Taylor from Designing Women. *These are two very funny people.*

My friend Lori Shelton went with me to Washington to celebrate Bill's inauguration as president.

I never saw Mother happier than she was during the inaugural week in Washington.

At the MTV inaugural gala with boxer Evander Holyfield.

After my performance with En Vogue, I spent time with Mother and Barbra Streisand.

Performing at the inaugural celebrations was one of the highlights of my career.

With Mother during our first visit to the White House.

With Molly, Bill, and Hillary at our wedding rehearsal dinner. I wish I could remember the joke.

Molly and me.

The best day of my life—March 26, 1994.

My brother and I sharing a wedding toast. He was drinking cider; I had champagne.

With my brother and Kenny G.

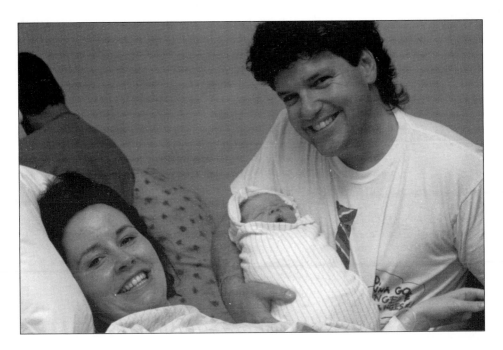

In the delivery room with Molly and newborn Tyler Cassidy Clinton—May 12, 1994.

Tyler and I at Redondo Beach. He was eight days old at the time.

Tyler meets his uncle Bill for the first time.

Tyler waves to me as I give a television interview.

Tyler can't run for president until 2032, but he already feels at home in Washington.

such as ring toss, basketball shoot, football throw, horseshoe toss, and softball throw were set up for the kids while they weren't playing softball. I shouldn't refer to the Special Olympians as kids, because many were in their twenties, thirties and forties. The looks of happiness on their faces if they won candy at the booths and the obvious excitement they felt at participating in the games warmed my heart. When they smiled or laughed, ran up and hugged me after hitting the softball, or grabbed my hand just to hold and squeeze it, I got chills. I also realized that the people who teach, counsel, and help the handicapped are very valuable and dedicated. I thanked God for so many things yesterday, but especially for those who help and love the handicapped. I feel fortunate and hope I never again forget to thank God for the many blessings He's bestowed on me.

DAY 233
Letter to Judge Harris, September 17, 1985

Judge Harris,
This letter is in reference to your upcoming decision on my Rule 35. I would like to say a few things in my behalf. It took me awhile to view my incarceration as anything but punishment. However, with a much sounder, healthier mind and body, I realize that my imprisonment was a necessity. It has been a blessing in disguise because truthfully I do not think I could have stopped my cocaine usage by a simple reprimand. Prison

certainly has not been as tough as it could have been, in actual conditions, but the loss of my freedom has been difficult to deal with. I have taken my freedom for granted, unfortunately, for most of my life, and being incarcerated has taught me the value of one's freedom. I have also come to sincerely appreciate the value of family, true friends, generous favors and gestures, whether large or small, and compliments as well as criticisms. From now on, I will try to never take anyone or anything for granted.

My attitude toward the use of drugs has drastically changed. Since arriving here at FCI-Fort Worth in February, my mental and physical states have improved greatly. I came here lazy and depressed, weighing two hundred and eighteen pounds, but I was determined to regain my composure. I currently weigh one hundred seventy-five pounds and look and feel better than I have in ten years, due also to the fact that I have not used any drugs. My mental state has progressed hand in hand with my physical improvement and I read frequently, keep a daily journal, write songs and poetry, and correspond with approximately fifty people on the outside. I feel renewed every morning when I wake up and every evening when I go to bed, and I don't ever want to lose this newfound feeling of control over my mind and body.

Hopefully, you will decide that I am ready to reenter society. I am anxious to work toward my life's goals and plan to strive for them with all my resources. It will take hard work, determination, and willpower to attain my goals while abstaining from drug use, but I know I can and will do it. I would like your faith, confidence, and belief in me to allow me to get on with my life.

A decision from you to release me from my remaining few months would be a tremendous confidence builder, and I would not let either of us down.

I have completed my drug programming, but am still taking three additional courses: insight therapy, a class on stress, and one on religious values.

When I arrived I harbored much animosity toward the world, but due to my therapeutic work here I have eased and virtually eliminated those feelings, including the self-destructive ones directed inward. I have become aware of certain negative character traits and habits that I have been able to discuss openly and work to improve upon. I have also found positive characteristics to capitalize on. The group discussions, augmented by frequent meetings with the prison psychiatrist and my counselor, have helped me in re-establishing my priorities, regaining my confidence, and redirecting my life in a more useful direction.

Spiritually, I have grown to a greater height than ever before. I attend church regularly and have taken two religion classes in order to learn more about God. Like so many other things, I took God for granted, but now I thank him every day, because I am still alive, despite my mental and physical self-abuse. God has certainly saved my life without question, but the reason why is still unclear to me. All I know is that He loves and trusts me, because He gave me this second chance at life.

There are many people who believe in me, Your Honor, but now I need for you to believe in me. I want to be released so I can start my life over.

Included is a copy of my progress report and a copy of a letter from a family friend in the Dallas area offering me steady, legitimate employment and a place of residence upon my release.

I thank you, sir, for your time and wisdom. I wish you well.
Sincerely,
Roger Clinton

DAY 246
September 30, 1985

It's about 2:00 A.M., so actually it's October 1, the day Judge Harris makes his decision on my Rule 35. I'm so anxious that I can't get sleepy, but perhaps writing this entry will help. I've eaten practically everything I could get my hands on tonight and just finished my third sandwich. I've been doing really well with my exercise-diet, so I guess I can afford to slip up one day.

DAY 269
October 23, 1985

Judge Harris denied my Rule 35 and I fell into a depression, which is why I haven't completed any entries since the end of September. It seems as though the "shorter" my time gets, the more anxious and less patient I become. I'm trying hard to control my irritability, especially toward the staff and the "system" in general. At any rate, my mother helped me realize that I'll be able to look back on this time and say that I did it all myself without a break from anyone. I'll try to look forward to that.

I met Wendy Sue R. on the first day of Autumn, 1985, Monday, September 23, and our first visit was the following Monday, September 30. We had a "date" the next Monday, October 7. She's a beautiful, sincere, intelligent twenty-four-year-old and we have so much in common. She's fun, funny, energetic, athletic, and, above all, emotional. I've sung to her during several rehearsals Bob, Dot and I have had, and she's very supportive of me and my proposed career. She gives me much needed love and confidence.

DAY 290

November 13, 1985

Good evening from my hospital bed. That's right. I'm in the prison's hospital and this is my second day. I was in too much pain to do any writing yesterday. I started feeling a sharp pain in my left side on Monday morning, but after a few minutes it went away, so I more or less ignored it. However, the pain recurred later that evening, and around 1:00 A.M., it had become so severe and wrenching that I honestly didn't know whether or not I was dying. I walked alone from my unit across the compound to the hospital where it took the officer five minutes to open the door for me. I could hardly stand up and was gripping my side because I thought it was helping. When he finally opened the door, I was seen by the physician's assistant, who asked a lot of questions. I could hardly speak to answer them and felt as if I were about to pass out. He asked for a urine sample which was an impossibility right then because of the tension and pain. I finally relaxed enough to provide one, after which the P. A. blessedly gave me a sedative. I fell asleep around 3:00 A.M., but woke again in excruciating pain at 4:30 A.M. No pain medication was administered this time, but I relaxed and went back to sleep around 5:30 A.M.

I awakened to a welcome sight—a doctor! An intelligent woman named Dr. Ballum has diagnosed my problem as kidney stones. I had an X ray taken, and tomorrow morning I am to be shot with a dye that will detail the size and location of the stones. Then I will see a urologist to determine what should be done. I have been praying that I won't have surgery, and I feel God will grant me that prayer. I know He was with me when the pain was the greatest.

Meanwhile, I'm praying for the pain to be over. I love my family, my friends, and my life forever.

DAY 291
November 14, 1985
At 11:30 A.M., I went down to X ray to let the radiologist shoot me with the dye that helps detect kidney stones. He had come from in town and knew what he was doing. That process took about an hour, and later this afternoon I was told by Dr. Ballum that they had located the culprit, a small stone. She said she wanted to keep me in the hospital through the weekend. However, if I pass the stone, I could leave the hospital.

Regardless, the pain inside me is not near as great as the love I have inside me tonight. I love you, Lord, for putting this love inside me. I love my family, my friends, and my life, forever. I love you, Wendy.

DAY 303
November 26, 1985

Good evening. It is approaching midnight, the end of what was to be my final day in prison, but due to my love for Wendy, plus the fact that I've always been a sentimental slob, I opted to stay an additional five days in order to spend Thanksgiving with Wendy rather than in a halfway house.

I passed my kidney stone and took it to the hospital for analysis. Tom Palmore found the "lost posters" that he mailed out for me (posters of his original paintings, which he auto-graphed) just in time to have them framed for Christmas presents. Wendy gave me something very special to her—a chain with a sil-ver whistle and a cross on it.

There was, however, some slightly negative news. I received my first incident report in the year that I've been here. I got caught eating lunch earlier than I was supposed to and having an early lunch card, which I hadn't been issued. I'm scheduled to leave Monday morning, so I don't think anything will happen.

My furlough was great! I got to see Lizzy, and she's always been so very special to me and always will be. I've loved her since high school. Together with Mike Pakis, Kim Sweatman, and sev-eral others, we had so much fun on my first night home. Lizzy and Mary Jane took me to Little Rock for a meeting with my attorney, Dan, before I caught a flight back to Fort Worth.

I have a head cold, and a million thoughts racing through my head.

DAY 308
December 1, 1985

Midnight of my final night at FCI-Fort Worth. I am but ten hours from release. I've washed all my clothes, packed, said my good-byes, and it's been a fulfilling, emotional day. There are several people here I will genuinely miss: Mark C., my tennis buddy and "best friend" here since Jaybird left, Mark L., who's got so much time it hurts me (five on an eight), Lew P. (his intelligence and sense of humor were my salvation many times), Tom P. (Apple-head, Saturn, etc.—an incredibly talented artist and a funny, off-the-wall, happy guy who was one of my favorite people). The main person I'll miss, though, is Wendy. She has been so wonderful to me. She's simply a beautiful person and has been a breath of fresh air in this stagnant world I've been living in the past year.

I was looking around today, taking notice of my surroundings for the past year. It's hard to believe that in a matter of hours I will regain my freedom, and immediately start to work on my new direction in life. I'm so anxious to do what I've always known I could do—be a singer! I'll try to live up to my final "Prison Proverb": Never brag on what you *can* do, unless you can brag on what you do! Amen.

CHAPTER FIVE

SWEET LIBERTY

"All my bags are packed, I'm ready to go . . . "

The refrain of that old Peter, Paul and Mary song wafted through my mind as I hurried to pack the last of my prison gear. I'd given away my most cherished possessions, like my nail clippers and my pillowcases. Suddenly, I noticed the guard outside the cell door. "What the hell are you doing, Clinton?" he asked brusquely. When I told him that I was packing to leave, he snorted with laughter. "Well," he said, "you can unpack. You aren't going anywhere."

For the first time since before my trial, I wanted to hurt somebody. I was mad at everyone then; mad at Bill for knowing I would be arrested but not telling me, mad at the state police for continuing to harass me, mad at God for letting me grow up with so much heartache, but mostly mad at myself for making my life a living hell. I have always had to work hard to quell my rebellious side, and it was especially difficult to deal with on December 2, 1985. For days, I'd been on an emotional high, counting the hours until I'd be a free man again. Most of the last few days I'd spent saying good-bye to special friends in my unit—friends I would never see again. Now, the prospect of freedom had been taken away—delayed for another thirty days, which seemed like an eternity.

Why? Because I'd eaten my lunch out of turn. Thirty more days for that infraction. I wanted to vent my anger somehow.

Some of the inmates in the cells alongside had taken the opportunity to steal chunks of fruit during mealtimes. They'd hide the fruit in their clothes, then sneak it back into their cells and place it in a large jar above the cell ceiling tiles for days. The result was a jar of fermented fruit and juice, prison alcohol. It was almost undrinkable, but not quite.

Time and time again, I'd declined offers to indulge in this jailhouse cocktail. "Now do you want a drink?" an inmate asked as he reached up into the ceiling and brought down the jar, thrusting it towards me. I took it without a word, unscrewed the lid, and held the jar up to my lips. The fumes alone were strong enough to knock me across the room, but I tilted my head back, raised the jar up, and let the juice and chunks of fruit slide down my throat. The stuff dribbled down the front of my prison shirt and was by far the worst thing I'd ever tasted. In my self-destructive moment, however, I didn't seem to care.

It took me two days to calm down enough to write another entry in my journal—the journal I had thought was finished forever. "I've been too shocked, too upset, and too bitter to write the past two days," I scrawled. "Again, however, the Lord has a reason for this or He would never have allowed it to happen." At the moment, it was difficult to imagine just what God's reason might have been.

I was sick and tired of being played with by the system, although to be fair, I had broken the lunch rule. Generally, though, I had tried to be a model prisoner during my year behind bars. Now I had another thirty days to get through, and I spent most of the time sitting in my cell. My blue window curtain was gone, as was most of my personal stuff. In a way, it was like being a new prisoner again, except this time, only a month stretched before me.

Only a month. God, how my family and I suffered through that month. I knew Bill and Mother shared the same heartfelt anguish when I wasn't released on December 2. Both had circled the date on their calendars; when it came, I didn't. "God help me," Mother wrote on her calendar when she received word I hadn't been released, "how can I stand more?"

⟶ CHRISTMAS IN PRISON ⟵

The worst thing about my extended stay meant I would be spending Christmas and New Year's in prison. To a family like ours, getting together for the holidays was an important tradition. Even after I'd been arrested, we still managed to see each other for Christmas. The thought of Mother, Bill, Hillary, and Chelsea spending Christmas together without me was almost intolerable.

As it turned out, the family didn't just spend it without me. They spent Christmas without Mother, too. Mother and her friend, Nancy Crawford Adkins, came to Fort Worth on Christmas Eve. They spent the night in a deserted trucker's motel, sharing a couple of bottles of liquor and eating Snickers bars from the motel candy machine. On Christmas day, Mother came to see me in prison. She said she knew she had to be there with me. Her visit was probably the best Christmas present I've ever had.

By Christmas day, I had been moved from my cell into a sort of alcove. The area was illuminated at night only by an exit sign. At midnight on Christmas evening, I sat alone and wrote another journal entry.

DAY 332
Wednesday, December 25, 1985.

Good evening on this most significant day of the year. Despite my location for this year's celebration, this day has been very special. Mother, Nancy, and Piper came to visit me today, so I was surrounded by love all day. Mother reminded me that at least I'm fortunate to have many more happy, wonderful Christmases to spend with my family. I topped the day off by calling and talking to Bill, but wished I'd been able to see him today. Despite all the negative aspects surrounding the delay of my release, there is a bit of positive irony. I'll be starting my "new life" at the start of a new year, so, needless to say, I'll need to have one helluva New Year's resolution!

After Mother went back to Arkansas, I started on the merry-go-round again. You go back to all the prison units you've utilized—the kitchen, commissary, library, chapel—and get the head of that department to sign your release card. Every department head has to sign off before you can be released.

I had done all this before, and I was familiar with the procedure as well as the attendant anxiety. Would I really be released this time? Would I ever get out? Would I be able to deal with freedom and the outside world? And how would I cope with the memories that remained?

Leaving prison is harder than you might think. It's a strange experience, reentering society after a year away. I knew that Mother and Bill would be supportive of me, and I knew I would never let them down again. But that was about all I was certain of.

I was unsure of how people would treat me, how I would react to law enforcement officers, and how the judicial system would affect me. It was essential that I do the right thing, for one misstep could land me back in prison facing my entire sentence. I didn't think I should go back to Hot Springs; it is such a small town, and I wasn't sure the people I knew would welcome me back into society with open arms. I decided to stay in Texas while I tried to make a new start for myself.

My time behind bars had been marked by three events. First was my initial night spent in prison at Texarkana. I shivered as my mind replayed the sound of the cell door sliding shut behind me. Another significant event was the day of my scheduled release. Even today, I cannot recall that day without powerful emotion. A third item of significance was the prison show I'd participated in. You haven't faced a tougher room than a main hall full of prisoners.

Could I still perform? Would they like me or hate me? The performance went well and the prisoners seemed to enjoy the show.

Many of my fellow inmates—and a few prison officials—had gone on to become friends. I would miss several people, like Herschal Robinson, my counselor at Texarkana. The reality of the situation—I would never relive these unique relationships—made my last few days in prison seem like the last days before high school graduation, excruciating but almost sweet because they would soon be behind you.

One big difference, of course, was that there are usually no reunions among prison inmates—unless they take place on the inside. And the inside of a prison, I told myself, was one place I'd never see again. I never once thought being in jail was a good thing. Years later, I had recognized that the cloud of prison had a silver lining. My year there had helped me grow and learn about myself.

Right now, though, I was preoccupied with making sure I would be in synch with the outside world. Except for transfers from one prison to another, I had been out of custody for precisely five days during the last year. First was a three-day furlough I spent with Mother, a girlfriend, Vicki Crawford, and Ricky Frazier near Shreveport, Louisiana. That first time away from prison was precious, and I wanted to spend it doing something Mother and I loved. We went to the racetrack at Louisiana Downs, where Ricky was a jockey. The second was a two-day furlough I took to Arkansas.

When the New Year came, I celebrated 1986 as a new beginning. I was still in prison, but I would spend all but the first few days of the year as a free man. I was proud of myself. I was surviving my ordeal and I was learning from it. It was time to move on.

⇢⇒ DON'T LOOK BACK ⇐⇠

I passed through the double doors of the prison as inmate 03210-010 for the last time. At the main building entrance there is another set of doors, and clerical staff sit behind a glass partition. I handed them my release paperwork; the warden signed me out. I did not shake his hand or thank him as prisoners do in the movies, just pushed the last door open and walked out onto the steps.

Mother was there to meet me. I collapsed into her arms and started crying uncontrollably. She held and comforted me. Piper Wilson had come to the prison with her, and when I finally stopped crying Piper guided Mother and me back onto the prison steps for a photograph. The picture shows us both with arms outstretched, thumbs raised high.

Mother headed back to Arkansas a couple of days after my release, but not until she'd taken me shopping for clothes and we'd had plenty of time to sit and talk about the past year. Despite all the phone calls and visits we'd had while I'd been behind bars, there was a lot of catching up to do. I called Bill the same afternoon I left prison and could tell from the tone of his voice that he was relieved the ordeal was finally over.

I was sorry to see Mother leave for home without me, but I wasn't ready to face Hot Springs and Arkansas. I didn't know what people would think of me; what they might say. I wasn't ready to bear the stigma of having been in prison. The fact that several of my so-called "close friends" had abandoned me on the eve of my incarceration did not bode well for a triumphal return home.

Mother could sense I was tense and insecure about coming back to Arkansas. "Nothing good comes easy," she told me, and I knew she understood. It would take some time before I was ready to come back home. I had a lot of things to work out on my own first.

I was sent to a room in a halfway house in downtown Dallas and lived there for four months. It was near the city's Central Expressway, close to the eastern edge of the downtown area. The halfway house had some pretty strict rules: Unless you had a job or you were looking for one, you stayed inside during the day. I got settled into my room and went out to look for a job.

Getting around the Dallas-Fort Worth metroplex on foot is daunting. The mass transit system was great, but it didn't go much further than the city limits. Again, Piper Wilson came to my rescue. She would either lend me her car, or she would drive me to job interviews. After a couple weeks of searching, I finally found a job working at a food warehouse in Grand Prairie, a thriving community about fifteen miles southeast of Dallas.

The Herby's Foods warehouse was huge—three levels jammed with boxes and crates from floor to ceiling. My job included operating a forklift and docking incoming trailers, but my responsibilities did not stop there.

The job was just what I needed, however, because it involved hard, physical work. The eight of us who drove forklifts at

Herby's worked twelve hours a day, unloading trucks and packing boxes. I eventually became very proficient at driving the forklift, but it took some time. I remember once raising the front end too high, and smashing into some long florescent light fixtures in the ceiling fixtures. Little slivers of glass rained down on my forklift cage, and the other drivers looked at me and laughed derisively.

At night, there was Piper. She'd be waiting for me when I finished work, and we'd spend a few hours together before I headed back to the halfway house. The next day, I'd start all over again. I didn't have time to turn around.

Keeping busy was a good thing, because I discovered my real enemy was idle time. I still like to sleep until at least 8:00 A.M. and sometimes be a television couch potato, but for the most part, I'm a workaholic. Too much time on my hands leaves me restless and frustrated, and I tend to become moody when I have nothing to do. When my mind is left to wander, it sometimes wanders over to the negative side of Roger Clinton. I'd never realized how dangerous that negative side could be until I found myself in prison.

Karen Ballard, a Little Rock therapist, had found this side of me during the counseling sessions Mother, Bill, Hillary, and I attended before I went away to prison. I had to learn to help myself past this negative side, Karen told me, or I could never hope to build lasting relationships and create a stable future for myself.

These counseling sessions helped the four of us explore our relations to each other, determine what had gone wrong, and develop strategies to repair the cracks in our family 's foundation.

We talked about every aspect of our lives together—my relation-ship with Mother and Bill, our respective relationships with Hillary, how Bill related to all of us. We didn't leave many stones left unturned.

I remember what a shock it was to learn that Bill had known of my impending arrest weeks before it happened. I had always been told he hadn't launched the investigation, and that he knew nothing about it until I was charged, both of which were com-pletely untrue. Bill had known of the investigation from the beginning and had been apprised of developments as it ran its course. Moreover, he had given his tacit approval. I was so mad at my brother—and at the world in general—I couldn't see straight. Just like that December day in prison, I wanted to hurt somebody. Now, however, that somebody had a name and a face. He was my brother, the governor.

Prison was difficult, but at least I was alive to do my time. Had I not been arrested, I might have died from cocaine because I was ingesting a lethal dose every day. At the time, however, I couldn't thank Bill for doing what he did. I was very, very sick. I wanted to deck him.

The decision to allow my arrest was very painful for him, and I know now he had no choice; after all, I was breaking the law. He couldn't tell anyone—not Mother, not Hillary—and he had to keep it all inside himself for weeks while the state police concluded their investigation and moved in on me. I understand the anguish he must have experienced, and I'm sorry I was the cause of it all.

I was suffering from low self-esteem, but Bill, Mother, and my friends kept telling me what a wonderful person I really was, and they insisted that I had to be a worthwhile human being because so many people loved me. I kept juxtaposing that with the turmoil in my life. There wasn't anything worthwhile about the fear, the need to escape, the constant tension, and—most of all—the unremitting loneliness I felt. If so many people loved me, I asked Karen Ballard, why was I suffering so?

Part of the problem, according to Karen, was that my actions had not been in synch with the kind of person I really was. I wanted to do things right, but I never did. The road to hell, I had discovered, was quite literally paved with good intentions.

After my release from prison, I finally realized intentions didn't matter as much as I had previously thought. Actions were more important, and if I didn't watch what I did, I could wind up back in jail. Late at night in the halfway house, I thought about those sessions with Karen, and I prayed to God to give me strength. It was no longer enough to want to do the right thing. My freedom depended on actually doing it as well. Looking back on those feelings now, I recognize them as somewhat adolescent in nature—the reluctance of a young man to take full responsibility for his actions, the tendency to be angry at the world for things not working out perfectly. Those were self-indulgent feelings, leading to self-destructive behaviors.

I stayed at the halfway house for four months, and worked at Herby's for six months. By the time I quit, it was the summer of 1986. Bill was up for reelection in Arkansas, locked in a rematch with his old nemesis, Frank White. Most observers had given White little chance of winning, but I could sense the mounting uneasiness in Bill, Hillary, and Mother as the campaign wore on. In 1980, I remembered, everyone had counted White out, and he had taken the election by a narrow margin.

Just before moving out of the halfway house, I made a trip to Arkansas to pick up my blue Mustang convertible. I wanted my own wheels in Dallas, and there were none better than the Mustang. I was weary of having to depend on Piper for transportation. Piper and I enjoyed spending time together, but she had her own life and I didn't want her spending so much of her time hauling me around.

Piper's family lived in Carthage, Missouri, a town about fifty miles north of the northwest corner of Arkansas. We'd known each other several years, but we'd lost touch by the time I went to prison. I only rediscovered Piper by chance, and having her in Dallas was a boon to me. Not only did she visit me in prison every Sunday for the last few months of my sentence, but she made it possible for me to live and work in Dallas when I was finally released. In my heart, I owe Piper a tremendous debt because she single-handedly helped me get through the initial transition from prison to the outside world.

I moved from the halfway house to my new apartment in the Candlewick complex on Greenville and the Lyndon Baines Johnson Freeway, known as the LBJ Freeway. Greenville Avenue is the heart of the north Dallas entertainment district and a busy part of town. It was a fairly hectic commute to Herby's from my new digs. In the mornings, I would edge the Mustang into the traffic on the LBJ Freeway, and drive bumper-to-bumper down to Interstate 35, which Dallasites call Stemmons Freeway. I'd head south on Stemmons, cross over onto Airport Freeway, and proceed west toward the sprawling Dallas-Fort Worth International Airport. At the airport exit I'd go the other way, turning south into Arlington, and then back east into Grand Prarie. At night, after another twelve-hour day, I'd drive all the way back home.

I guess people wonder how someone can drive an hour each way to work, work twelve hours, and still have time for a social life. My energy level was high and had been since I was released from prison. In addition, I was staying in good physical shape working at Herby's, and I don't remember feeling tired from the exertion at all.

During the long summer of 1986, I began to reapproach my musical career. There are many clubs along upper and lower Greenville Avenue, and I auditioned for the chance to perform in some of them. Getting up in front of a cosmopolitan Dallas audience for the first time was a new experience in stage fright. As it turned out, the crowds were kind, and throughout the summer I sang at places with exotic names like Cardinal Puff's and Popsicle Toes. Those experiences helped me put to rest any doubts about trying to build a musical career.

As fall drew closer, I felt a strong urge to return to Arkansas even though I had conflicted emotions about facing my friends back home again. Nevertheless, I went. As much as I hated to leave Piper, the Greenville Avenue clubs, and the glitter of Dallas, I also wanted to go back to Arkansas.

I had no thoughts of picking up my life where I'd left off when I went to prison. Instead, I moved to Mountain Home, Arkansas, a small town near the northern border of the state. There, I took one of the least interesting jobs known to man: cash register clerk at a General Quik-Mart.

While Bill Clinton was being elected to a fourth term as governor of Arkansas, Little Brother was busy stocking shelves, taking inventory, and ringing up customers in a Mountain Home convenience store.

Mountain Home was half a state away from Hot Springs, so going home to see Mother meant a four-hour drive. As it was also a considerable distance from Little Rock, I didn't spend many weekends at the Governor's Mansion. The place had a kind of solitude about it, and the isolated piney woods of northern Arkansas promoted reflection.

⤖ A RETREAT TO THE WOODS ⤗

Despite its remoteness, Mountain Home offered me opportunities to perform in public at outdoor concerts and events. These bucolic venues were not as classy as I'd seen in Dallas, and the audiences I played to were vastly different from the sophisticated, urbane club-goers of Greenville Avenue. Some of these events were sparsely attended, others drew huge crowds. Either way, I got up on stage and did the best I could. Most audiences seemed to appreciate my efforts, and I was grateful for that.

I was even more grateful for the realization that, as I'd done in Dallas, I could play my music straight, without the use of drugs.

I stayed in Mountain Home through 1987 and, to this point, it was the calmest and most peaceful year of my life. No fighting parents to listen to, no drug deals to make, no prison bars locking me in at night. Above all, I was developing self-discipline and following a routine.

It really didn't matter that I was working at a convenience store because I was proving to myself I could follow the schedule. I got up at a certain time every morning, worked my shift, and did what was expected of me. At night, I went back home and worked on my music. Sometimes I had to force myself to keep the routine going. That's why I stayed in Mountain Home for more than a year; to make sure I could maintain that level of self-discipline.

By late 1987, I was certain I could handle living on my own. It would be more difficult in a less isolated place, I knew, but I had to try. I packed up the Mustang and headed to Little Rock.

I wanted to spend more time working on my music, of course, but I would also need a day job, and I wanted one that would offer some challenging physical labor and get me outdoors. Through a series of fortuitous circumstances, I ended up on a bridge construction crew.

In Little Rock, I joined Alcoholics Anonymous, and my sponsor, Gene Walter, arranged for me to meet a man named John Lawrence. We hit it off, and I moved in with him and his wife,

Anno, and went to work for his sons who owned a highway bridge construction company.

The construction job was daunting—we worked ten to twelve hours a day, six days a week, in all sorts of weather. The distance between the Lawrence home and the construction site forced me to get up very early each morning just to complete the drive and be at work on time. I drove from John and Anno's house in Maumelle, an upscale bedroom community west of Little Rock, through the capitol city itself, then down through Benton on the highway toward Hot Springs. Each evening I'd make the drive back to Maumelle. I lived by the clock, trying hard to be punctual.

My first day on the job site, I nearly blew it. We were working on a stretch of the old Benton Highway and the foreman handed me a bucket of nuts and bolts. I was to walk across a six-inch catwalk that ran alongside a highway bridge and put the nuts and bolts in place on a metal support structure.

The danger in the assignment was evident. I didn't have any experience with heights. It was too high off the ground to be working on a piece of steel.

Rebellious feelings welled up in me and I almost said, "I don't have to take this crap." The words were on my tongue, but I kept my mouth shut. Instead, I turned around and carefully made my way across the bridge.

The job was an incredible breakthrough for me. I worked hard, became a good employee, and learned something new every day. Just doing the work day in and day out was a huge accomplishment.

Since Mother's house was just a half-hour down the highway, I could have had a battle on my hands. Someone or something might make me mad—a foreman would tell me to do a job over, or give me another menial task to perform—and I could begin to get angry. The madder I got, the more I might think about chucking the whole job and hopping into the Mustang. I could be at Mother's house in minutes. She could take me in again, I knew.

The truth is I didn't really want to run; it was just a reflex. I'd actually begun to like the work. I enjoyed the disciplined cycle—the early commute, work, lunch, more work, the drive back home, evening AA meetings. I was proving to myself—on a daily basis—that I could work in society again.

I was also beginning to enjoy being around people again. John and Anno Lawrence were great to me. They lived in a very large house on a golf course in Maumelle. It was peaceful and quiet; a beautiful place for me to come home to at night. I remember Mother saying that her only worry about my new job was that John was a Republican.

Mother would drive out to the job site some days at noon to bring me a sack lunch. Soon enough, she started bringing sandwiches for some of the other guys as well. We'd spot Mother's car from our vantage point high atop the bridgework, and we'd bound down the grassy slopes to meet her and gather in a field next to the highway where she would pass out sandwiches. Mother seemed to enjoy being in the middle of the laughing and joking construction workers. After eating, I'd spend a few minutes alone with Mother. We'd lie back on the grass, looking up at the big, open, Arkansas sky. We didn't say much to each other—that beautiful sky said it all.

Mother had married again some years after Jeff's death to a food broker named Dick Kelley. I was largely ambivalent about the new marriage, and I found that Dick was largely ambivalent about me. He thought—quite correctly—that I needed to grow up. But he was there to give Mother strength when I went to prison, and I was grateful for all the times he drove her to visit me in jail. After my release, I found I enjoyed spending time with Dick. He sensed I was finally growing up, and he welcomed my new-found maturity.

Bill drove through the construction site once, just to see how I was getting along. He didn't get out of his car, but I knew it was him, and that was what really mattered. If he had gotten out and walked over to talk with me, it might have affected my relationships with my supervisors and my co-workers. I didn't need that sort of attention, and Big Brother knew it.

He was beginning to think that I was no longer wasting my life. Bill has always had a deep respect for manual labor. I knew I was on the right track when he began showing a renewed interest in what was happening in my life. He'd call me more and more often, ask Mother how I was getting along, and he watched me as I took the first few steps toward reestablishing my musical career.

One day I got a telephone call from Vaughan Reed, who had been the bass player for our old band Dealer's Choice some years back. Vaughan was out in Nashville, working with country music star George Jones. Vaughan was in charge of selling

George Jones T-shirts and merchandise during his concerts, and he needed help.

It was a nice opportunity and a heady prospect—being on the road with a recording star. I was tempted to take the job and run, but I didn't. I was just beginning to get my life back together and I figured I wasn't ready to move to Nashville yet. I did, however, finally move out of John Lawrence's house and into a small rented house in western Little Rock, near the intersection of two main avenues, Markham and University. My roommate was a friend named Matt Jacuzzi. I met Matt at Hendrix, and I was close to his parents. Matt's family is well-known for spas and hot tubs. Matt had two wonderful sisters whom I also knew well.

I continued to work at the construction site every day, and in the evenings Matt made sure I didn't have any idle time. I played basketball and we worked on our music together. Other nights I would attend Alcoholics Anonymous meetings.

One evening, the telephone rang again. It was Vaughan Reed; the opportunity to work with George Jones was still open. Some months had passed since Vaughan's first call; enough time to make me feel that I had my life back on track. I was ready to try something new, and I really missed the music.

I told Vaughan I'd take the job and then began the process of sorting things out and getting ready to move. I had to help Matt find a new roommate, give notice at work, and let my probation officer and AA brothers know what I was doing. Bill and Mother seemed happy that I was finally going to put the past behind me and do what I really wanted to do.

What a year 1989 was turning out to be! I was happy with myself and what I was doing with my life. The memories of my time in prison were fading rapidly, and the old demons of drugs and addiction were even further behind me.

Late one evening I loaded up my new "used" car, a maroon Nissan Maxima. The next day at dawn I slipped out of Little Rock before the rush hour. I hit Interstate 40 and headed east, bound for the Tennessee border, Nashville, and George Jones.

CHAPTER SIX

HOORAY FOR HOLLYWOOD!

"Hold onto your table," Vaughan shouted to me from across the hall, "here they come!"

The last notes of "He Stopped Loving Her Today" were greeted with wild applause from the concert-goers. Suddenly, the auditorium doors flew open and a surge of humanity headed straight for me. George Jones fans swarmed around my merchandise table like a plague of hungry locusts, buying tapes, albums, and T-shirts with wild abandon. I took their money hand-over-fist, wondering if there would be any merchandise left to hawk through the bleachers.

Even if selling George Jones products wasn't quite the music-career breakthrough I had envisioned, I still managed to learn from the job. A lot of what I know today about managing a successful stage production I learned from that time with George Jones.

When I moved to Nashville in the fall of 1988, it was still a busy, bustling show town and the only place to be in if you were in the country music business. Branson, Missouri, was not yet on the map as the country music Mecca of the world.

A friend turned me on to a guy named Peter Moret who had recently gone through a divorce and was now looking for a roommate to share his house. Peter was a terrific chef—he could cook red beans and rice better than anyone I knew. He worked at Opryland U.S.A., the big country music theme park in Nashville.

I arranged to split the mortgage payments with Peter, and we moved in my couches, tables, bedroom suites, and my stereo system to furnish the house. As it turned out, I would be there only for about a week every month, but the arrangement with Peter gave me a nice home to come back to after time on the road.

Selling merchandise for George Jones was *hard* work. During each concert, Vaughan and I had just a few minutes' time to get tapes and T-shirts to ten or fifteen thousand people. When we were under the gun to clear out our inventory, we ran the bleachers of the auditorium, yelling and selling. If you ever ran bleachers in gym class, you know it doesn't take long for that kind of exercise to get you in really good shape.

We would all be dead tired after the shows, but instead of heading to some motel for a few hours' sleep before heading to the next town, we slept on the road in one of George Jones's two buses. One was for the exclusive use of George and his wife, and the other was reserved for the road crew. Our bus slept a dozen of us, with bunks arranged in tiers along the middle of the aisle. In the front of the bus, just behind the driver, there was a lounge with two bench seats and a table. At the rear there was another lounge equipped with a stereo, tables, and couches.

The people managing the tour valued money more than anything else. I've since learned that's what good managers are supposed to do. They worry about money while the star worries about performing. Because the focus of the tour was to generate cash, everything else was secondary to that objective. Everyone, I learned—except George himself—was expendable.

Vaughan spent a week or so showing me the ropes of the merchandising industry. The merchandising end of the tour had mostly been in Vaughan's hands for the past eighteen months, and prior to that time had been handled by George Jones's sons. Bobby Burkhead, George's road manager and drummer, took it over from them and, with Vaughan's help, he managed to double the gross in less than two years. When I first came on board, the merchandising operation was just beginning to boom. That's why Vaughan needed me; there was enormous market potential for us to tap.

⤙ LIFE AS A ROADIE ⤚

Our first show was in Texarkana. Vaughan kept me beside him as he worked his table, and we were so busy I jumped in and helped him sell that very first night. We worked side-by-side for a month or so, with Vaughan showing me how to manage crowds, how to focus on one transaction at a time, and how to prepare the table for the next intermission. We had been out on the road a month or so when Vaughan gave me my own table.

George's real strength was performing songs with a message he really felt. One of my favorites was "He Stopped Loving Her Today," which is a sad ballad about a man whose love for his wife stops only when he dies. George sang two songs, "We Can Make It," and "The Race Is On," that attested to his can-do attitude and never-say-die spirit. When Merle Haggard performed with George, they would often sing a duet of "Yesterday's Wine," a song with personal resonances.

After the show, the entire crew headed backstage. The take-down and load-up of the set required time and manpower, and Vaughan and I often helped once we had finished stowing our merchandise. Occasionally, I tried to spend a few minutes back in the prep area with George and the band. People from the audience with backstage passes would also be milling about in this area waiting for George to walk out of his dressing room, wave to the group, and thank them all for coming. He has a unique way of making each person he talks with feel incredibly special, and if you were backstage, you could meet George and walk away feeling as if you had connected with him.

From time to time almost any performer gets upset with the technical people. There are minor glitches—sometimes major ones, too—because each show is a complex combination of talents and technical wizardry. From time to time, you see some performers become visibly upset when things aren't going their way, belittling their support team sometimes even from the stage itself.

George seldom did that. He had a way of communicating that inspired us to do things his way, and he never berated us when things went wrong; he just accepted the mistake and went on with the show.

Onstage, George was just a country boy, talking to an audience of folks who'd grown up just as he had. He could make people in the audience feel as if they'd known old George Jones all their lives, and that is why he's so loved and respected today. His record sales speak volumes about George's ability to touch an audience.

He took to calling me "Scotty." I had a habit of pulling my sweatpants up to my knees, exposing knee-length socks. I guess I must have looked something like knickered golfer Payne Stewart does on the golf course, although perhaps not quite that snappy. However, I dressed for comfort, because we would ride in that bus for hours at a time. When a man like George Jones gives you a nickname, it's usually a sign of affection, so I was happy to be "Scotty" instead of Roger.

Bill didn't know George, of course, but he encouraged me when I told him I was going to take the job with the tour. "I know you can make good things happen for yourself," he told me. He wished me all the luck in the world, and he tried to encourage me that the simple path to success consisted of learning all you can.

I think Bill realized—much more than I did at the time—that if music was to be my career, learning from someone like George Jones was an incredible opportunity for me. Of course, I didn't have to ask my brother to support my decision to join the tour—I could have been selling T-shirts, warming up the band, or sweeping the auditoriums for all he cared. If it touched the music world, Bill was for it.

On our first major tour early in 1989, we headed north to Canada. We stayed on the road for a solid month, playing at stops all through Ontario. Then we headed east to Halifax, Nova Scotia. What an incredibly beautiful place Nova Scotia is! I loved the country and the people. Most of us on the tour had the time of our lives, the bitter cold notwithstanding.

We headed down through Maine, and I got to sample real Maine lobster. Today, I'm trying to get my wife Molly to share my fondness for it, but I'm not making much progress. Her culinary adventurousness ends with a bowl of clam chowder.

Further down the East Coast, we entered the heart of George Jones country. In Virginia and the Carolinas, where his most ardent fans live, people went wild. This was a great part of the tour for me as well; the mountains and forests to the west reminded me of Arkansas.

We were on the road two hundred days of the year, but every three or four months, I would get a week or so off. Vaughan and I would restock the warehouse and take inventory, then he'd tell me to clear out for a few days. I'd head back across Tennessee toward the Mississippi, then into Arkansas. Little Rock was just a few hours away from Nashville; Hot Springs another few minutes beyond. I always went to Mother's first, and spent some time with her. Mother loved what I was doing, even though she wasn't really a country music fan, apart from of the affection that every Arkansan holds for stars like Patsy Cline and Glen Campbell.

During these visits, Mother and I would spend some time at the Oaklawn racetrack. We never won or lost a lot of money there, keeping ourselves in check by placing only two-dollar bets. We'd spend the entire afternoon watching the ponies run and we both loved the atmosphere, the excitement, and our friends there, but we particularly liked being together. Mother would sit beside me, wearing the gold racehorse necklace I'd given her. I didn't always see Bill on these return trips, but one time he did drop by the racecourse with television producer Harry Thomason and the security entourage in tow.

Working with George gave me the music bug, worse than I had ever had it before. The yearning to perform seized me. On the way back to Nashville, I would drive through Memphis and often stop on Beale Street to visit a club called Rum Boogie. I knew the man who owned the club, Don McMennan, and he would let me sit in with the band. I treasured those side trips to Beale Street, and I loved the jam sessions, the smoky clubs, the funk music. I sang at one or two other Memphis clubs, but I always came back to Rum Boogie.

Back in Nashville in the fall of 1989, we prepared for the state fair circuit. George made quick hour-long appearances at fairs across the country. It was a fast-paced tour, and the money was good. People at fairs are always in the mood to spend, and Vaughan and I did a land-office business at each stop along the tour. We met some good folks and hit the midways and the wildest rides when we could.

Conway Twitty and Merle Haggard often toured with us. Conway toured with us on most of our city-to-city trips, and he was there for the state fair tours as well. George would open the show. When Merle was with us he'd close it.

The musicians themselves were all great guys and top-notch professionals. Eventually, I started warming up with the band, which was as close as I could get to performing onstage in front of an audience. Before the doors opened and the crowds started pouring in, I'd head to my merchandise table where Vaughan and I would brace for another onslaught.

I think that my time with the band—and the time I spent listening to George sing—helped me develop a real appreciation for country music. I know that country music is sometimes viewed by other kinds of musicians as a celebration of low-class tragedies that all sound the same. You've probably heard the old joke: Spin a country record backwards and you get your wife back, your dog comes home, and the repo man brings back your pick-up. That's a simplistic view and I like to think of country music in a different way. To me, country has a simple message. The music itself is a voice showcase—that's why so many country stars are such outstanding vocalists. They have to make the music work.

I think country performers genuinely enjoy what they do—unlike some popular artists I know. Out of every thirty songs I work on personally, I'd estimate five or six are country "crossover." On my first compact disc, I had one song—"Ain't No Cure for You"—that was close to being a crossover from popular to country. I'd eventually like to do an entire album of crossover music.

I've never attempted anything close to pure country music, except perhaps on demos or cover tunes, but I love the style, the challenge, the message, and the utter beauty of country music. People who sneer at country songs don't know what they're missing.

As we plowed through the 1990 state fair circuit, Bill was making his final bid for governor. He had an easy time in his fifth gubernatorial race, and I think Mother and I both expected he would try to run for president in 1992, although we were careful not to look ahead to the next race until the last one was safely behind us.

I was at home in Nashville one August afternoon when Mother called.

"Can you help me through a crisis?" she asked, her voice calm. Crises were a normal part of growing up Clinton.

Mother's disclosure stunned me.

She had gone for her annual physical examination, and her doctor, John Haggard, had found a lump in her breast. After consulting a surgeon, Dr. Haggard told Mother he wanted to operate on her the next day. She told him she needed forty-eight hours. Then she drove home, called Bill at his office, then called me.

I tried to hold myself together, telling her everything would be all right. I promised her I would come home that evening. Then I hung up the phone and fell apart.

I simply lost control, collapsing on the couch and crying for what seemed like hours. I was in shock, scared, and feeling the full weight of Mother's agony. Finally, the realization dawned on me that I couldn't help her sitting in Nashville and crying. I left immediately for Arkansas.

A day later, doctors performed a mastectomy. Bill, Dick, and I were by her bedside when Mother woke up after the surgery. I think I knew her ordeal with cancer had only begun. "We just have to be strong and pull ourselves together again," Mother told us.

The day after the surgery, Mother put on her makeup and started roaming the halls of the hospital. She spent her time with Bill, Dick, and me, and she enjoyed talking with former medical acquaintances she hadn't seen since retiring in 1981.

During this time, I was grateful I was no longer a worry for Mother and Dick—that she didn't have to mother me any longer. Instead, I was holding and comforting her. Days slipped past before she finally convinced me she was going to be okay without me at her side. I went back to Nashville and got on with the tour.

I talked often with Mother and Bill during that fall and spent Thanksgiving and Christmas with the family. Bill had won his bid for reelection as governor with 59 percent of the Arkansas vote. "I have looked into the eyes of the people of this state," he told his supporters early on the morning after the election, "and I have seen a yearning to do what is right and best for the children, to move forward."

I was feeling the same yearning to move forward, to do what was right for Roger Clinton. If and when the opportunity came, I wondered if I'd be ready for it. Just after the turn of the year, I sat down with Bill and told him about my desires to begin performing onstage again. "I'm ready now, and I think it's time," I told him, and he agreed with my self-assessment. "I want to do whatever I can to help," Bill told me. I knew he meant it, but at that moment, I couldn't think of anything he could do to help me break into show business.

January 15, 1991, was Bill's inauguration day. The ceremony, which had always been held on the state capitol steps, was moved inside into the legislative chambers because of rain. I stood beside Mother as Bill put his left hand on the Bible, raised his right hand, and took the oath of office for the fifth time as governor. After his inaugural address, the celebrations began.

I had the opportunity to sit in with a group called The Grown-Ups, which performed at the inaugural ball. The group formerly went by the name Main Squeeze, and they still perform in Little Rock today under their new name. I enjoyed singing to a hometown crowd, especially since the last time I'd performed in Little Rock had been years before. Prior to my arrest and jail sentence, I'd sung a few times at a rather classy restaurant called the Brown Bottle. Singing with The Grown-Ups was like coming home again.

After our second set, a young man walked out of the crowd and up to the stage. I knew him; he was a Little Rock optometrist named Danny Thomason.

"Man," he told me, "you're the blackest-sounding white guy I've ever heard. I'm going to tell my brother about you."

I knew Danny's brother, of course—I had met Harry Thomason some months before when he and Bill came to the Oaklawn racetrack in Hot Springs. I knew Harry did something in Hollywood, but I didn't know what. Also, I didn't know that Linda Bloodworth was Harry's wife, and that as a team they were one of the most powerful forces in Hollywood.

I stayed in Arkansas a week before I headed back to Nashville. When I got back to the house I'd been sharing with Peter Moret, Harry Thomason had called. I called him back.

"My brother says you should be out here," Harry told me. "I can help you get started." It developed that the work would be manual labor, helping take care of Harry and Linda's aircraft in their Los Angeles hangar.

I sat back for a moment and thought about moving to California. If I was really serious about making it in music, I at least needed to be where the music business was.

⇒ CALIFORNIA, HERE I COME ⇐

Initially, though, I was reticent. "I don't know anybody out there," I told Harry. "I don't have any place to live."

"We'll worry about all that when you get out here," Harry told me. He had already made up his mind—I was coming to Hollywood.

"All right, Harry, I'll do it," I told him, before I had really thought about what I was saying.

"Call me when you get into town," Harry said. Then he hung up.

I stared at the telephone. I had just committed myself to moving to California. There was notice to give to George Jones, people to see, dozens of things to do before I could be on my way.

Back in Arkansas, it was hard to say good-bye to Mother and

Bill. Bill was excited, of course—I was going to work for a good friend of his. He knew, as I did, that I had to start somewhere.

"If Harry and Linda can't help you in the entertainment industry," he told me, "nobody can."

Mother was happy for me, but the thought of us not seeing each other as often was painful for us both. What really concerned me was Mother's illness. She had already started chemotherapy, and the treatments would continue through the summer.

"I'm fine," she repeated often. "Don't worry about me." I knew she was trying to keep her attitude positive and her spirits high.

I said good-bye, jumped into my Nissan Maxima, and drove to Dallas to spend a couple of days with former Scully Street neighbors Will and Donna Schubert. While I relaxed with Will and Donna, I had a good talk with myself. In reality, I decided, I had been putting off moving to the West Coast for the past five years. I had to be where music counted, I told myself. Sitting in the Schuberts' living room, I decided to stop looking for all the reasons not to go and to focus on the good things that could happen to me in California.

It took three days to make the drive west. I would drive several hours each day, stopping along the way when something interested me or I grew sleepy. As I drew closer to the Los Angeles area, I noticed the huge electric transmission towers, with their miles and miles of wire cable stretching down the side of the highway toward the horizon. I entered Los Angeles, and blindly followed the road signs toward Hollywood. I had no idea where I was.

Finally, I swung off the highway. At the bottom of the exit ramp was a 7-Eleven store. I stopped the car, got out, and carefully locked the door behind me. You can't be too careful in the big city.

On the front wall of the convenience store was a pay telephone. I dropped in my dime and punched Harry Thomason's office number.

It took a few minutes for the secretary to get Harry on the telephone. When he answered, I breathed a sigh of relief. When you've driven for days to get to a city where you know practically no one and have no place to go, you can be pretty anxious. "Harry," I said when he picked up the phone, "Roger Clinton here. I just got into town."

Harry had news for me.

"You can still go to work at the hangar," he said. "But...."

A production assistant's position had opened up on the *Designing Women* set. Harry was candid with me when he described the job.

"Nobody working for Linda or me would want this position," he admitted, "but everyone else getting started in Hollywood would kill for it."

He wound up his pitch by telling me he'd heard I was great working with people, and I'd be a bigger asset to him and Linda if I worked on the set.

A production assistant is essentially a glorified "gofer." You run errands for anyone and everyone on the set and you take care of personal odds and ends for the cast.

Designing Women was a hit situation comedy based on several women characters launching an interior decorating business. Delta Burke was hailed as the star of the show when I joined the production team. Dixie Carter played her sister, the brains of the operation. Annie Potts, Meshach Taylor, and Jean Smart made up the rest of the ensemble.

The first time I walked onto the set, I was awestruck by the amount of equipment and the apparent confusion caused by so many people running here and there. I was lost, and fearful of breaking something. Quickly, I learned my way around the set.

I learned my way around the studios and the neighborhood streets when I took Harry's car to the car wash. I learned about the players and their relationships with the Hollywood community. I learned about production timetables when I delivered Linda's scripts, and watched, quiet and fascinated, as they taped the show once every week.

Happily, I remembered I *did* know someone in Los Angeles besides Harry and Linda. Gene Short, a Hot Springs neighbor, had married Kathy Altenbaummer, who had grown up a couple of years behind Gene and me. Now they lived in Ontario, about forty-five minutes outside of Burbank.

I moved into their spare room, which had been converted into a sort of office. We reconverted it by moving in a folding cot for my bed. During the first few days in California, I was not certain that things would work out, and Gene and Kathy gave me a safe haven while the other aspects of my life got sorted out.

It was an hour-and-a-half drive from Gene's house to the studio. I got up before dawn every morning to be at the studio by 7:30 a.m. I would work a twelve-hour day, drive another hour-and-a-half back to Gene's, and sleep for four or five hours before I got up to do it all over again. I was living on adrenaline, and the job was so exciting I didn't miss the sleep.

I stayed with Gene and Kathy for two or three months before I finally got my own place. I was so wrapped up in my work that searching for an apartment wasn't a high priority. Eventually, however, I found a one-bedroom studio in North Hollywood on Toluca Lake. Calling it a "studio" apartment might be stretching the truth a bit; actually, it was a converted attic space in an older two-story home.

Still, I was glad to find it. The landlady was a bit eccentric, but I was close to both Warner Brothers in Burbank and Studio City. It was just down the street from Bob Hope's home, and I stayed in that attic apartment for a year and a half before I found something larger.

I guess I stayed so long because I didn't spend much time there. I was moving into the Hollywood social scene, so I wasn't home on weekends. My days on the set—especially Thursdays— were very long. The apartment served its purpose as my bedroom, if not as a place where I spent much time.

The show was pretty much my life during this period. Every day on the set, as I ran errands and fetched coffee, I worked at getting to know Harry, Linda, and the rest of the cast. People often ask me to describe Harry Thomason, and I tell them he's a big teddy bear. But sometimes that teddy bear becomes a grizzly. He's powerful, and occasionally ruthless, but in Hollywood, ruthlessness goes with the territory. Harry has as big a heart as anyone I've ever met, not to mention an incredible amount of talent and patience—two qualities not often found in a single individual. He knows show business like virtually no one else in Hollywood, and he's very loyal to his family, his friends, and the shows he produces. Harry would happily go to the wall to keep a show of his on the air.

Linda Bloodworth-Thomason is a creative genius. She can be very quiet and introverted, especially when she's doing something out in a crowd. She watches people and pays rapt attention to what she sees. On the set, she is dominant—very powerful, very confident, and very imaginative. She has a take-no-prisoners attitude that—along with her creative talent—has put her at the top among the Hollywood producers. Linda is the kind of person you want working with you and not against you. In that respect, she's a lot like Hillary.

Both Harry and Linda work hard, longer hours every day and every week than anyone I've ever seen—except Bill. As a team, they are passionate and tireless, and they seem to draw a lot of strength from each other.

Harry and Linda have become more than friends to me; rather, they provide a mental, moral, and emotional orientation without which I would be lost. I consider Harry my dear friend. He appointed himself my guardian, and I feel I can trust them with things I can't tell anyone else. When Mother died, they were my anchor. During her illness, they did everything they could to alleviate her suffering. He and Linda flew Mother out to Colorado so that she could investigate some experimental cancer therapies. Mother rejected the therapy because living in isolation for six weeks—as the process required her to do—wasn't living to her. I know that she deeply appreciated what Harry and Linda were trying to do for her, but that sort of therapy wasn't her style.

"You tell my boys I'm doing fine," she told Harry before she flew back to Arkansas.

One day while I was working on the set, Harry stopped me in a corridor.

"Roger," he said plainly, "I don't know anything about music. But the security guard down the hall is a musician. He plays some kind of horn. Why don't you go down and introduce yourself to him?"

I walked down the hallway and shook hands with D. A. Bookman.

Like most musicians, D. A. had a day job—security guard at Warner Brothers' Studio. He played the saxophone, and he performed in a band called Sun Bear. Ahaguna Sun was on drums. The guitarist was a guy named Werner Schuchner. Everybody called him "Bear."

When I could, I would go to clubs and listen to D. A. and the guys play. They were good—very good. And one day, when I was working on the *Designing Women* set, The Idea came to me.

⊶ THE IDEA ⊷

The Idea focused on the studio audience. Whenever a live television program is being filmed, several hundred guests are sitting high above the set in arena-style seats. They watch the action on the floor and on the monitors that hang from the ceiling. Of course, this sort of audience is essential to the actors, particularly in comedy. The performers feed on the energy generated by those watching the show as it's being taped.

The audience response is taped as well, and played back as part of the show's television soundtrack. Members of the audience come from everywhere. Some are tourists, others are friends of the production crew or the stars. One night, we even had a studio audience contingent from a local halfway house.

The production relies on a professional actor to "warm up" the audience, so the crowd will be in the mood to laugh and have a good time during the sit-com taping. Since taping a show can take three or four hours—or more—someone works with the audience during the set changes and breaks to ensure that no one gets bored.

My thought was to have a band entertain the studio audience during these breaks. This would take some of the stress off whoever was doing the warm-up and it would give the audience a chance to listen to upbeat music during the long pauses between scenes. I had the perfect band in mind—D. A., Sun, and Bear with Roger Clinton singing lead vocals.

One day, I walked up to Harry.

"Normally," I joked, "I don't really audition. I send out tapes."

Then I explained the idea to him. "This would be perfect for us, and perfect for the audience. If you don't like it, if you don't think it will add to the studio entertainment, that's okay."

If he did like it, I told him, we wanted to be paid for performing every Thursday night.

The four of us got together and rehearsed. We needed a new name, something that would reflect the tone of our show, the times, and the lead vocalist. We decided to call ourselves "Politics."

I wasn't particularly nervous when we performed for Harry; I knew we were going to be good. Harry hired us, and we started warming up audiences on Thursday night. Those evenings became a mindless blur for me, as I was still also working as a production assistant. To prepare for the musicial performance, I would talk with the director and study the shooting script to spot the set changes, wardrobe changes, and production breaks that signaled a performance from "Politics." We had our repertoire of songs ready to go.

I would "go-fer" on the floor through the taping and run like mad back to our little platform when the breaks started. The band would perform, then I'd run back downstairs onto the studio floor to do my production assistance job.

The audiences liked us. The warm-up man would introduce us, and away we'd go. We did some classics, like "Suzy-Q," "Ride, Captain Ride," and some original compositions that later appeared on my first album. While eating up the music, the audience would also slurp down the ice cream we'd help hand out during the breaks.

After Bill had announced for the presidency, some member of the audience would ask the warm-up person if I was Bill's brother. A lot of the time, the question was meant as a joke—something clever to say. When the warm-up person replied in the affirmative, the audience would turn toward our platform and stare at me. It was strange to be the object of such curiousity simply by virtue of being related to Bill, but I must honestly say that I kind of enjoyed the spotlight being in such a position cast upon me. Later, there were times when that extra attention would be more annoying, but at the beginning, it was an interesting novelty.

Designing Women continued to occupy one of the top sit-com slots and was usually in the top-ten-rated shows every week. The show was great, and I was getting to know the stars. Dixie Carter, who played one of the Sugarbaker sisters, is the epitome of a southern lady, and I felt very much at home with her, just as I did with Harry and Linda. I became friends with Meshach Taylor and Jan Hooks. Delta Burke, who is incredibly talented, kept me laughing constantly. Then there was Annie Potts. A beautiful brunette, a magical actress, and a wonderful personality all rolled into one, Annie really charmed me. She had already starred in films like *Corvette Summer, Pretty in Pink,* and *Ghostbusters* before she came to *Designing Women*. I guess it's obvious, but I think Annie is one incredible woman.

As the summer of 1991 wound down, I took a little time to reflect on the recent and dramatic changes in my life. I had gone from Nashville to Hollywood and was living and working in the entertainment Mecca of the world. I had a job I liked and new friends; my brother was serving his fifth term as governor of Arkansas, and best of all, Mother's cancer had apparently gone into remission.

Also, the West Coast press had finally decided to leave me alone to live my own life. Of course, I'd still be mentioned in the Arkansas newspapers whenever Harry and Linda would visit Bill, or when some society columnist got word that I'd made a trip back home. A negative description would generally follow any mention of my name, no matter how neutral the context. "Governor Clinton's brother, Roger, who was convicted of cocaine distribution . . . " was how it usually went.

The media still couldn't bring itself to mention me without also mentioning that part of my past. Finally, I had gotten to the point where it didn't really matter to me anymore by discovering that I had the power of choice. I didn't have to listen to what the media said about me. I could choose to tune it out and turn it off, and that knowledge was a real liberator for me.

Harry and Linda taught me not to let the little things bother me. I had also learned to control my temper. By the fall of 1991, I could take any ball that was handed to me and run with it. That was a good thing, especially as Bill was going to run for president.

Funny thing is, Mother and I had been expecting him to run for the past four years. We thought he was ready in 1988—but he wasn't. We were certain he'd throw his hat into the ring in the fall of 1991 or in early 1992.

Most of my friends considered the next presidential election a foregone conclusion. George Bush had just won the Persian Gulf

War; his popularity ratings were high, and there didn't seem to be any way a Democrat could unseat him. Conventional wisdom held that if Bill ran, he'd get some good experience in a national campaign. According to the armchair political quarterbacks, he didn't stand a serious chance.

But I knew my brother better than they did. I knew then—and I know now—that it's always a mistake to count Bill Clinton out; to say he has no chance to win. The timing was right, Mother and I thought, for a Bill Clinton political miracle. He'd win, we knew, just because no one thought he could. He'd surprise them all.

CHAPTER SEVEN

BROTHER, BROTHER

On October 3, 1991, Bill announced that he would run for president of the United States.

Harry Thomason and I flew to Little Rock a couple of days before Bill was scheduled to make his announcement. We all knew he was going to announce his candidacy, of course, but the local newspapers played up some sort of "mystery" news flash.

The announcement site was Little Rock's Old State House, the first Arkansas state capitol. Built in the Greek revival style, it's an imposing building with a large courtyard that holds several thousand onlookers. We all felt it was the ideal place for Bill's big day.

Mother and I were tremendously excited. If she had any doubts, she never voiced them to Bill or me. Back in the summer, she had told a reporter she wasn't sure whether she wanted Bill to run for president.

"One day I do, one day I don't," she said then.

Now, any lingering doubts any of us may have had were long gone. On the morning of the announcement, Bill radiated confidence. This was the right thing to do.

The media turned out in full force. The three Little Rock television stations had trucks on the scene, and stations from across the state and as far away as Memphis and Shreveport sent reporters to cover the event. The three national networks were well represented. Mike von Fremd was there from ABC, and NBC sent producer Collette Rooney. CNN had camera crews on hand as well. Television networks as far away as Australia and Japan would be picking up the satellite feed from the Little Rock stations.

Mother and I were going to get our first taste of national and world media coverage.

Bill had already endured the bite of the national press with his ill-fated Dukakis nominating speech in 1988. He'd even done Johnny Carson's *Tonight Show*. However, this would be a new thrill, or perhaps a new ordeal for Mother and me. Our mistake lay in thinking we were prepared for it. Within minutes of the announcement, it seemed, the media declared open season on the Clinton family. For the next thirteen months, we all lived in the unremitting glare of the public spotlight. The scrutiny didn't end with Bill's election to the presidency; if anything, it became only more intense.

Of course, both Mother and I had campaigned for Bill prior to his announcement. We talked about Bill with people we knew, using our friends as a sounding board, often asking them what they thought about the national political situation. We'd get their opinions, and then we'd tell them about Bill.

Bill had been out doing some opinion-gathering of his own. He talked with voters across the country to get their impressions of where the country was heading. If he'd found that most folks thought the nation was on the right track, he wouldn't run.

What he found was that most people thought the United States needed some sort of dramatic turnaround. Bill saw a divided America, and he began to see how he could bring the country together. He knew he could make a difference and help the country move forward.

There were those who thought his candidacy ill-timed and ill-advised. "George Bush," one newspaper columnist wrote, "towers over this election like a colossus." Quite a few of the pundits seemed to believe that any Democrat was wasting his time running for president. Their convictions didn't dissuade us in the least. Mother and I not only thought Bill could win, we were dead certain that he *would*. Bill is a people person and, in this country, people elect presidents. His strength is talking to people, campaigning face-to-face, and telling the truth. He works incredibly hard at politics, and people see that.

He had also mastered politics—it was his craft. He was sincere, hard-working, personable, and charismatic. People responded to him, and he connected to them. The combination of his extraordinary intelligence, his work ethic and discipline, and his knowledge of the political arena made Bill a tough presidential contender.

Mother and I had watched him for so long, waiting for this moment. It was like watching a professional ball player grow up. Most pros are natural-born leaders, and they excel at every stage of their game. As we watched, Bill had grown into the part.

We'd been wearing custom-made buttons for months. "Bill Clinton for president of what?" people would ask us. "Wait and find out," we said in reply. We bided our time and waited for Bill to tell us the race was on.

⋙ THE RACE IS ON ⋘

At 10:00 A.M., Little Rock police closed off the streets surrounding the Old State House. The fall sun was shining brightly as we drove the few blocks through Little Rock to the Old State House. The eighty-degree weather, bright sunshine, and perfect blue sky gave the morning an unreal, dream-like quality. Bill was scheduled to speak at noon. Mother, Dick, and I walked across the fenced-in courtyard, and settled into the bleacher-like VIP seats to the left of the speaker's platform. Hillary stayed with Bill, while Chelsea sat on the steps of the building, talking happily with some of her grade-school friends.

The speaker's platform was ringed by a dozen American flags. Another high platform, this one holding several television cameras and crews, jutted up in front of the podium. While the national television audience could see the action, the cameras and their platform blocked the view of many Arkansans who had come to hear their governor announce his candidacy.

About thirty-five hundred Clinton supporters crowded in the courtyard around us. The program began at 11:00 A.M., and the Hope High School band was on hand to entertain us. After the invocation, Harry Thomason got up to say a few words. Then Jimmie Lou Fisher Lumpkin, the state treasurer, introduced my brother.

For the first time, Mother and I heard someone call Bill "the next president of the United States." Watching Bill walk to the podium after that introduction was one of the most exciting and electrifying moments of my life.

His speech lasted thirty-two minutes. About a third of the way through Bill made it official. "I proudly announce my candidacy for president of the United States," he said, and a massive cheer went up across the courtyard along with a barrage of "Clinton for President" signs.

Bill finished his speech and took time to work the crowd, shaking hands with those who had come to see him and wish him well. Fleetwood Mac's "Don't Stop Thinkin' 'Bout Tomorrow" boomed from the courtyard loudspeakers. Friends crowded around Mother, Dick, and me. I was caught up in the emotion of the moment and waded into the sea of faces, shaking as many hands as I could.

We all went into the Old State House after the announcement. Mother and I hugged Bill, praising his speech. Then we got into our cars and headed back to the Governor's Mansion. Bill and Hillary had a fund-raiser that afternoon, and Bill had dozens of news organizations waiting to interview him. For all of us, but especially for Bill and Hillary, the long journey to the White House had begun.

I stayed in Arkansas for another week before returning to California, spending most of my time with Mother in Hot Springs. Bill hit the road, leaving two days after the announcement for a speech in Iowa. A day later, he addressed the American Israel Public Affairs Committee in Dallas and the following day flew north to New Hampshire, the all-important first primary state. He hit three more cities that week. That weekend, I saw him in Los Angeles.

Back at work, I noticed that everyone expected me to be a changed man. The people and circumstances surrounding me might be changing, but I wasn't. I didn't know how to be anyone other than who I was.

Then the press showed up. By the time Bill was the Democratic front-runner, the media was omnipresent. My friends and co-workers endured the onslaught with patience and courtesy. On the set, they were kind to my new status as brother of the Democratic nominee.

Our first assistant director, William Cosentino, and the second assistant director, Les Banda, worked hard to keep the media from disrupting the show schedule. "Coz," as I called him, was really supportive. He is a very serious, competent, capable professional, and he helped me handle my obligations to the media with true professionalism.

The camera crews would troop onto the set, unpack their equipment, and shoot B-roll of me playing with the band. I'd do interviews during breaks in the show shooting schedule. Sometimes, the cameramen would want to rework my hair and put makeup on me before they shot their interview. *The Designing Women* cast put up with the intrusion, and I appreciated their tolerance.

"What's it like," the reporters would ask, "having a brother running for president?" Now, how in the world are you supposed to answer that? He was the only brother I had, so I didn't have much basis for comparison. I answered inarticulately, I'm afraid, replying that I had a great deal of pride in Bill, and that I felt a huge satisfaction in watching him campaign. I added something about feeling excited and overwhelmed at the same time.

⊷ THE PAPARAZZI DESCEND ⊷

In late January, a supermarket tabloid printed allegations that my brother had engaged in a twelve-year illicit relationship with a former Little Rock nightclub singer. The vocal minority—the small percentage of the press who didn't care about Bill's ability—jumped at the chance to push Bill Clinton out of the race.

He survived, although this was clearly a large hurdle both personally and politically. The naysayers seized upon the draft issue. The draft issue was something akin to whipping a dead horse. Vietnam was history: You can't saw sawdust. Bill had simply voiced his opinion, in protests and in his letter to one Colonel Holmes, remaining true to his convictions that the war was not in the best interest of the United States.

Then came the marijuana brouhaha. None of these negative campaigns worked. His opponents had underestimated Bill's ability to communicate with people, and they had overestimated the public's interest in Bill's personal life. Still, the media brought more stories forth—some of them bought and paid for.

I also faced the daily firing squad known as the press. They beset me with questions about Bill, which I fielded as best I could. In the end, all I could do was tell them what I believed, nothing more. The media circus around me only increased in intensity as the spring of 1992 wore on. I actually felt their presence keenly enough to wonder if my "celebrity" status was an intrusion to the *Designing Women* cast. Everyone continued to go out of their way to make me feel as comfortable as I could, under the circumstances. Nonetheless, I felt hounded wherever I went.

The pressure was unrelenting. I often spoke for Bill at fund-raisers and special occasions. I performed for free in Sacramento and Los Angeles, closing my performances with a short speech in Bill's behalf. I felt a great sense of pride in speaking in Bill's behalf.

I spent as much time as possible actively campaigning for Bill. I couldn't quit my job to work for the campaign full-time— Bill wouldn't want me to do that. In some ways, I could do more for his effort by staying where I was and letting the press come to me.

Reporters continued to press me, although the requests for interviews seemed to run in cycles. The amount of time I spent talking to reporters declined after Super Tuesday's primaries, picked up again before and after the convention, fell off again until after Labor Day, then hit again with a vengeance.

After Super Tuesday, I needed a break and headed to Arkansas for some time with Mother. As usual on visits, we went to Oaklawn racetrack to watch the ponies run. Even with the media swirling around us both, it seemed the natural thing to do. As I was walking through the crowd carrying drinks for Mother and myself I ran into an old friend, Gay Campbell. Gay had been telling me for some months that I should meet a friend of hers. Today, the friend was with her, and I said hello to Molly Martin—a brunette with warm green eyes, and a lovely smile.

That night, I met Gay and Molly at a place called Marguerita Bay in Hot Springs. This is a popular Mexican restaurant and nightspot on the lake. On the deck overlooking the water, we sat and talked through the evening. Molly lived in Dallas, and I quickly resolved to plan a trip to Texas. As it turned out, Molly and I would soon develop a close relationship despite our geographical differences.

Back in California, Linda was in almost constant contact with Bill and Hillary, helping them fine-tune their television appearances. Harry would fly to Arkansas or wherever Bill happened to be campaigning. He insured that Bill made a positive appearance during major televised campaign events and literally took charge of staging the Democratic National Convention in New York City, where Bill would become the party's candidate for president.

I wanted to be there, of course, but not just as a spectator. I didn't want to ask my brother if I could perform, but I wanted to do more than spectate as events unfolded.

One day Bill's friend Randy Goodrum called me. Randy had been a member of Bill's jazz combo, "Three Blind Mice." "Roger," he told me, "I've got a song I want you to listen to." I went to see Randy, and together we sat back and listened to "Circle of Friends."

The song captured the spirit of Bill's campaign so perfectly, there seemed only one place to perform it. "Let's form a circle of friends," the lyrics said, "one that begins and never ends." Randy had me picture Madison Square Garden in my mind, and then he helped me fill the mental picture with cheering convention delegates. I saw myself walking out on stage and singing his song, while everybody in that huge arena held hands. The visualization was so real to me that I could have reached out and touched the faces in the crowd.

I went to Harry Thomason, who was helping stage the entertainment at the convention. Randy had told me, "You have to sing this song," and now I shared his conviction with Harry. This was the right song for the right place, I told him.

It took me a couple of months to convince Harry, but I pushed the song relentlessly, finally selling him on the beauty and simplicity of its message. He passed the idea on to my brother, who approved it. I would sing the song with Jennifer Holiday at the very end of the convention, after Bill had made his acceptance speech.

Selling this song to Harry, then actually performing it at Madison Square Garden, marked the first time I had been a part of something like this from the ground up. I had started the ball rolling, been persistent, and now I would see the process through to completion. It was a terrific honor and a thrill, but it was more than that. This song was a tribute to Bill and all that he had accomplished.

I arrived in New York as the convention got underway on Monday, July 13, 1992. Mother and I were staying at the Intercontinental Hotel, in midtown. As a family, our schedule in New York was tight—there were parties, get-togethers, cookouts, and delegation meetings to attend. We spent a lot of time with the Arkansas crowd, of course, but our main function as the family of the nominee was to circulate among all the state delegations. Mother and I pressed the flesh just as we had back home. I kept telling myself that this time the nomination for the presidency of the United States was at stake.

⟨⟩ THE COMEBACK KID ⟨⟩

On Wednesday evening, we sat in Madison Square Garden and watched as the delegates nominated Bill for president. He walked out on stage shortly after the balloting. Since the rules of the convention didn't allow him to accept the nomination of the Democratic Party that night, he would wait until Thursday evening. Then, he said, he'd officially be the "Comeback Kid" that so many in the media had been calling him.

It had been a long road. Nine and a half months had passed since Bill threw his hat into the ring, and he and our family had been through a lot. We all knew, though, that the most difficult part of the journey still remained—the fall campaign.

Late on the final afternoon of the convention, after I'd rehearsed "Circle of Friends" with Jennifer, I went back to my room at the Intercontinental, showered, and put on a loose-fitting gray suit. I wasn't nervous; I don't usually get nervous when I'm about to perform. Instead, I get excited. I knew that singing in front of such a huge crowd would be one of the ultimate experiences of my life, and I wanted to soak up their energy and give it back to them. I wasn't worried about anything. Tonight would be the pinnacle of our family's life to date, and I knew I would start blubbering while on stage.

On Thursday night, Mother and Dick watched Bill's acceptance speech from the family section in Madison Square Garden, while I was backstage. Early in his speech, Bill stopped to thank Mother for all she'd done. More than anyone else, Bill knew, she was responsible for this moment.

One writer called the final evening of the convention an "overlong altar call," and it was a summons, although I personally didn't think it was too long. Bill was summoning the Democratic Party faithful to share his vision of America, just as John Kennedy had in 1960. Time and time again, he was interrupted by riotous applause. The entire speech lasted something over an hour.

When Bill finished, the convention was over. All that remained was the entertainment and the closing ceremony.

Jennifer Holiday went on stage to begin the first verse of "Circle of Friends" and I listened from backstage. Since we hadn't had much time to rehearse much that week, we had never even thought of trying to choreograph the song. During the rehearsal earlier that day, how we would stand on stage was something neither of us addressed. We would both just walk out and sing.

I walked up behind Jennifer as she finished the first verse. From the side of the stage, someone handed me a microphone. I took three steps forward and started singing the second verse.

The interior of Madison Square Garden was awe-inspiring. The Clinton/Gore banners waved from thousands of hands, and everything seemed to slow down. The crowd, vibrating with heat, distorted the sound and the music for me. The song came out perfectly, but my mind was reeling.

"There's way too many people out there hurting," I sang. "Doesn't anybody care about the pain?" I raised the microphone and gestured to the delegates to join us in the chorus.

Mother, Bill, Hillary, and Al and Tipper Gore appeared out of the corner of my eye as I finished my verse. Jennifer and I started the chorus, and the stage began to crowd with people.

The crowd was still cheering and screaming, but people were holding hands now. Delegates were singing the chorus with us, and the stage became more and more crowded. The crush of people was so great, Jennifer and I couldn't move at all.

As we closed the song, the crowd went wild. Twenty-five thousand people exploded into cheers and applause, and a sea of Clinton/Gore signs filled the arena. Mother and Bill were still on stage, applauding with the delegates. Jennifer and I thanked the crowd, then I went back to sit beside Mother until the convention was officially brought to a close.

The next morning, I returned to California and got back to work. Ross Perot had withdrawn from the presidential race—for the moment, anyway—and I had said good-bye to Bill and left New York certain that the tide was swinging in our favor. If you believed the polls, we had the election sewn up.

Of course, November was more than three months away. A lot could happen between now and then. I was still confident Bill would win, but I wasn't ready to begin celebrating just yet. I recalled the congressional race in 1974, when we went to bed thinking Bill had beaten Hammerschmidt, but awoke to find that Bill had lost. In 1980, we knew the election was slipping away, and it did. Those two experiences taught me a lot about the volatility of campaigns and elections.

I was always more concerned with the trends shown by polls than with the percentages and numbers, although of course we paid some attention to the numbers. Bill had a huge lead in the polls coming out of the convention, which was to be expected, but that lead evaporated following the Republican Convention. The race seemed to begin all over again after Labor Day. I often thought of the home stretch—this period from Labor Day to Election Day—as a test to see which candidate could make the least mistakes.

In the late summer, the media began drawing comparisons between me and Billy Carter. For the most part I found them amusing and could see where the obvious comparison was coming from, although we shared very little except our status as male sibling of a presidential candidate, and later, of a president. Billy Carter was represented by the media as something of a beer-guzzling fop, but the truth is he was an unselfish and complex man. Likewise, they saw me as a former drug addict trying to manufacture a career by cashing in on my brother's fame and power. Both are narrow and unfair interpretations. I tried to see that Billy Carter's generousity wasn't overlooked by the media; there' s little I can do to rectify my own negative image other than prove it false.

When Billy had been diagnosed with a terminal illness, he decided he wanted to do something to help those in similar situations. At his own expense, he travelled across the country talking with people who were facing their own mortality. He counseled and lectured on terminal illness and helped suffering thousands face the inevitable result of their illness.

I took it upon myself to tell the story of Billy's final months to the press in an effort that was unsolicited and unauthorized. Every time someone would make the comparison between Billy Carter and myself, I replied with the unsung story of Billy's efforts to help others. Billy himself was unconcerned with his legacy.

I have nothing but respect for Jimmy Carter. Bill always told me that he was a brilliant and gracious man, and when I met President Carter at Bill's inaugural, he thanked me for what I had said in his brother's behalf. It was a generous and kind thing for President Carter to do.

The media, which had fostered negative story after negative story about Bill during the primaries, now shifted its attention to President Bush. Some of the negativity toward my brother disappeared, although a good bit remained for the last two months of the campaign.

I always thought three things would help unseat George Bush: the confirmation of Clarence Thomas as Supreme Court justice; his changing stand on the abortion issue; and finally, the implications of the Iran-Contra affair. It seemed to me that too many people were implicated in the Iran-Contra affair for President Bush to disassociate himself from it without political repercussion. The appointment of Clarence Thomas—and the resulting controversy with Anita Hill—had essentially divided the country. By his own admission, President Bush had shifted from a pro-choice position to one disallowing abortion. I thought at the time—and I think today—that enough voters were on Bill's side of those three issues to swing the election toward Bill. I also think even George Bush would tell you he was dealing with the strongest politician he'd ever faced—Bill Clinton.

After Labor Day, Bill would call me often. "Rog," he'd ask, "what are people out there saying?" and I'd give him my assessment of the concerns and expectations of the voters I'd talked to. People in the entertainment industry wanted new leadership from someone who was vibrant, alive, and would work hard to solve the nation's problems. "All our friends are very optimistic," I'd tell him, knowing the news might cheer him but wouldn't affect him. Postive feedback just made him work harder.

Bill was an indefatigable campaigner. I've never seen anyone in modern politics take the sort of verbal battery and physical wear and tear that Bill endured during the fall of 1992. The harder Bill worked, the more he got in touch with America. After the convention, he was within reach of America's needs and desires. By the time of the three presidential debates in October, I felt that Bill had his fingers firmly on the pulse of the nation.

I watched the debates carefully, focusing not just on the three candidates, but on the audiences as well. This sort of confrontation—a dialogue between himself, his opponents, and the voters—was Bill's forte. I think he really scored points with many voters during the final debate. Meanwhile, the polls continued to favor us, albeit by slim margins. But with Ross Perot back in the race, the contest was too close to predict with certainty. All we could do was wait for November 3.

I flew to Arkansas a couple of days before the election. Mother and I spent the day before the vote campaigning around Hot Springs and Garland County. The one state Bill could be sure of, most people thought, was Arkansas. Mother and I were going to make sure that assessment was correct. We voted in Hot Springs, then drove to polling sites around the county to make sure that Clinton supporters had everything they needed. Toward late afternoon, Mother, Dick, and I returned to Little Rock.

Bill was still at the Old State House, awaiting the latest exit polls. Exit polls are interesting things: They can predict trends and give you a ballpark idea of what to expect as the final result.

But the problem is that some people won't respond to exit poll-sters. Consequently, there is always some skew to the numbers.

We headed for the Clinton/Gore campaign watch party at the Camelot Inn, which overlooks the Arkansas River in down-town Little Rock. Everyone was excited and upbeat, and Mother and I thanked them for a job well done before proceeding to the Mansion to meet Bill and Hillary.

Bill had been on the campaign plane until the early morning hours, with stops in Denver and in Fort Worth. Despite that sort of schedule, he seemed energetic and anxious for the returns to start coming in.

The first results came in from the northeast, which was con-sidered a George Bush stronghold. We were either winning most of the states, or we were very close. As the minutes ticked by, we gathered momentum and began to outdistance the incumbent.

BIG BROTHER, THE PRESIDENT

I think most people would expect a moment of high rejoicing when President Bush conceded the election to my brother. Certainly, we were happy to hear his speech, but I think most of us were overcome by the solemnity of the moment. Bill had just been elected to one of the most powerful offices in the world, and I think all of us watching at the Old State House felt the burden of responsibility as it descended on him.

Before Bush's concession speech, we motorcaded across town to the Old State House, the site of Bill's candidacy announcement more than a year earlier. An enormous crowd had gathered outside the venerable old building, overflowing the courtyard and the streets beyond. Our family and the Gores entered the building through the back entrance. Mother, Dick, and I walked to the front of the building and stood at the side of the steps for a little while, enjoying the excitement of the crowd and talking with old friends. Then we went back inside and stood behind Bill as he acknowledged the victory.

When Bill finished his speech, Mother and I moved up alongside him, Hillary, and Chelsea. The Gore family joined us as well, and we spent several minutes waving to the crowd in front of us. It was certainly a moment—and a night—to remember.

I went back to the Camelot, where many in the campaign staff were celebrating the night away. Stephen Stills, a big supporter of Bill's, was entertaining the ballroom crowd. I was standing out in the ballroom with some friends, listening to Stephen play his guitar and sing. Suddenly, he leaned into his microphone and looked directly toward me. "Come on up here, Rog," he said, "and help me with this next song."

I was so excited, I thought I would wet my pants.

He didn't need to ask twice. I scrambled up on stage while Stephen continued to strum his acoustic guitar. When I was ready to sing, he started playing "Teach Your Children."

That song—a favorite of mine—was the perfect cap to an unbelievable evening.

The next day, I took time to reflect, thank God, and let the realization take hold. We had so much to be grateful for—that we had all summoned the physical and mental stamina the campaign required, that we, and especially Bill, had had the ability to stick to the course. In Little Rock, the media and people on the street were celebrating the election as well. Better than anyone else in the country, Arkansans knew where we had come from, and where we were going. My brother walked to a breakfast the morning after the election, and the crowds surrounding him were incredibly friendly. They were admiring, too—and a bit curious.

"Now that you're president," one lady asked him, "do we have to call you Mr. President, or can we still call you Bill?" My brother laughed along with everyone else. What people chose to call him was the least of his concerns.

Mother gave an interview that afternoon. She was asked by a reporter if she was as excited now as she had been during the campaign. Bill would be leaving for Washington and wouldn't be around very much. "He's not going to be as accessible," the reporter said, "and you've got to be sad about that."

"Not at all," Mother replied. "He's been mine for forty-five years, and now it's time for me to share him with the world. That doesn't make me sad at all—it makes me happy."

I thought it was a wonderful response.

It took me a week to come down to earth and get back to work. Back in California, I found the whirlwind no less intense than it had been in Arkansas.

Now that I was going to be First Brother, people were even more interested in me. There were always reporters and camera crews interviewing me at work; again, the staff and my friends on the set were wonderful about letting me spend time with the media. I guess I feel ambivalent about the attention, some of which I enjoyed—I hadn't asked for it and there was little I could do about it.

Some months before Bill announced his candidacy for the presidency I had talked with several record companies about my music. My lifelong career goal, of course, was to have my musical talent recognized and appreciated. Recording an album was—and is—the most direct way to accomplish that. I would be white-washing my own motives unless I admit that I took advantage of some of the opportunity coming my way in the fall of 1992 as a result of being Bill's brother.

Despite the fortuitous circumstances, I still believed in my own ability to perform and entertain. A long time ago, I had rid myself of the notion that I had to be the best musician on the planet. All I had to do, I told myself, was be the best I could be. I continue to grow and improve every day, and that's the most I can ask.

There's always room at the top for talented individuals who like to work hard and are honest. My chances to make it to that elevated status were greatly enhanced by my brother's election, no doubt about it. I feel that I would have been a fool to pass up the opportunity.

Christmas interrupted my new activites and I flew to Arkansas in late December to celebrate Christmas before Bill, Hillary, and Chelsea moved into the White House. That time with my brother was very emotional, as it represented a significant shift in the pattern of our lives together. Mostly, we sat and talked about how our lives would change. Bill made it clear he wanted to maintain the strong family ties and he'd be as accessible to Mother and me as he could.

At the end of the day we drove back to Hot Springs. Hillary and Bill stayed at the Mansion with Chelsea, although they came down to Mother's a day or so later.

We could not know it, but this would be the last Arkansas Christmas we'd spend with Mother. Her cancer had returned and this time there would be no remission. Christmas 1993 would see her enjoying the Yuletide at the White House, and I'll always be glad she had the opportunity to experience that sort of joyous holiday.

In Washington, preparations were underway for the inauguration on January 20. Mother and several of Mother's best friends were planning trips to see Bill sworn in as president. I would be there, too—entertaining at the MTV ball, the Arkansas ball, and an acoustic set on the Monday before the inauguration.

January 20, 1993, was a Wednesday. I was staying at the Mayflower Hotel. Mother and Dick, along with Dick's brother Al and his wife, Nancy, were in the presidential suite. By the time I got out of bed that morning, I could look out the window and see thousands of people on foot, walking down the mall toward the Capitol to be there when my brother became president of the United States.

It was bitterly cold on the platform outside the Capitol. I sat with Mother in back of the podium with Hillary's parents, Hugh and Dorothy Rodham. Lori Shelton had come to Washington with me, and she sat a few rows behind us with Linda and Harry. We waited for Bill's arrival; then suddenly he and President Bush were walking down the wide aisle toward us. Hillary and Barbara Bush sat down together in the front row.

We sat through the invocations and Maya Angelou's poetry, then watched with pride and awe as citizen Bill Clinton became President Bill Clinton. The actual oath of office is less than forty words, but it felt monumental that day.

A moment later, we were on our feet applauding. Bill flashed Mother a look of heartfelt gratitude. Then, in his first act as president, he turned to the podium and delivered his inaugural address.

As I listened to Bill, I looked out over the immense crowd. The sea of people was a breathtaking sight. Minutes later, when the Air Force jets and the helicopters flew overhead, saluting Big Brother, unbidden chills ran up and down my spine.

That afternoon, after Bill and Hillary walked down Pennsylvania Avenue, Mother, Lori, and I went to the White House. Pictures of the building had not prepared me for the grand splendor of the place. Suddenly, there we were—driving up the driveway. In a sense, it was our family's home now. We walked inside and upstairs to the family quarters where I was surprised to see the movers had gotten so many of Bill and Hillary's things unpacked already. The place didn't look bare, as you might have expected. We had a snack in the solarium and then, bushed, I went to lie down.

I fell asleep in the Lincoln bedroom; that is, on Lincoln's bed. I'll remember that bed as long as I live. It's a beautiful old piece of furniture, with marvelous styling and a gorgeous head-board, if a bit short. That afternoon, as tired as I was, I thought it quite comfortable. Harry and Linda Bloodworth-Thomason would sleep there that evening.

I got up, ate with the family in the solarium, then returned to the Mayflower to change prior to the MTV inaugural celebration.

At the MTV ball, the attendees were all from the entertain-ment industry. The head of Atlantic records was there. Yikes! The label had just signed me, and I'd be performing for him. Some of the people I met included: Carl Lewis, Tommy Hearns, and Evander Holyfield. Mary Steenburgen, the actress from Little Rock and already a friend, was there as well. And, I was honored to meet Shirley MacLaine.

I was scheduled to sing a single song with En Vogue, one of the top groups both in chart rankings and money earned. A per-formance by 10,000 Maniacs preceded our act, and Don Henley followed us.

We performed the old Sam Cooke tune, "A Change is Gonna Come." I was oblivious to everything else except the music and my performance. This wasn't like performing at another Bill Clinton fund-raiser; everyone had come for an evening of enter-tainment. I was as excited as I've ever been and it was a new high in my musical career.

The performance was an incredible honor for me, and an incredible opportunity as well. It didn't hurt that the MTV gala was being televised live across the country.

When the song was over, I stood in the television lights for a moment, savoring the applause. Then, some of the production assistants escorted me off the stage and out to Mother's table. Beside her, in a shimmering gown, sat an attractive blonde. I'd never met this woman before, but I recognized her immediately.

Mother motioned for me to sit down next to her. I leaned across the table to say hello to Barbra Streisand.

It was that kind of night.

CHAPTER EIGHT

DIFFERENT MAN

Nineteen ninety-three was a wonderful year, a year filled with changes. Bill, Hillary, and Chelsea were ensconced at the White House. I traveled the world performing that year, and my record deal moved a step closer to reality. I took several punches in the media and delivered one or two myself. Molly moved to California, and we soon learned we were expecting a baby. Jim Moore and I took the first steps toward writing this book. Most importantly, our last holiday season with Mother was filled with happiness and excitement.

When I returned to California following the inauguration, I knew none of what was in store. Mainly, I was concerned with how Bill and I would manage to keep our relationship going. We had talked often throughout the campaign, but I felt that things were different now. For everything a president does means there's something else he cannot do. He'd have less time and more pressing things to do than call me. I didn't want to lose touch with Bill altogether, but I didn't delude myself—nothing, including my relationship with my brother, would ever be the same.

Amazingly, Bill kept up his routine of calling me once or twice a week. The important thing was that our relationship—and our ability to communicate with each other—didn't suffer due to the demands of the Oval Office. When Bill calls, he doesn't just pick up a telephone and dial out; the White House switchboard places the call for him. Each call out is logged, of course, and made on a secure phone line. Once the operator gets you on the phone, the call is transferred to the president. Depending on what Bill is doing at the time, I might have to wait a few seconds or several minutes for him to pick up the phone. If I call him, I simply tell the White House operator I want to speak to my brother. Bill gets the message and he calls back when he can.

One evening after I'd recently returned from a trip overseas, I called the White House to let Bill know I'd made it home safely. Since he was scheduled to deliver his State of the Union message in an hour's time, I didn't expect a call back until much later in the evening. He surprised me by calling back almost immediately, wanting to talk.

"How was your trip?" he asked. "Tell me about it."

His concern for me was unflagging, even when he had far more important things to do. Once I used my cordless phone to carry on a long conversation with my brother. After we rang off, my dog and I went for a walk. My neighbor came out into his front yard to say hello.

"You just talked to your brother at the White House," he told me.

I asked him how he knew.

"Easy," he replied, "I listened to the whole conversation on my baby monitor."

If White House phone protocol took some getting used to, it was nothing compared to my First Brother status. The media onslaught continued, but now news organizations and reporters came from all over the world rather than just from the fifty states. Some wanted me to come to them, and several times I took the opportunity to see the world and share information about Bill at the same time.

One of these involved a three-day trip to Barcelona for a television interview. On the set, you wear an earphone so you can hear your interviewer's questions translated into English. You can't pay attention to what you're hearing in your left ear; you must focus on the interviewer to your right. Your body language must convey a falsehood—you want to look like you understand what he's saying. Your reply is then translated into the host's language. It's a very tedious process and it takes a lot of concentration to make sure the interview "looks" right. I found the process interesting, even though the foreign journalists ask the same questions reporters here in the United States do.

I wish I had a dime for every time someone asked me—in any language—what it's like to have a brother who is president of the United States. Everyone everywhere wants to know about the trials and tribulations of Bill's campaign—Gennifer Flowers, the draft issue, the marijuana flap. Hillary is also a subject of curiosity all over the world. "What is she like?" people ask. "Is she pushy and demanding?"

I always describe Hillary in glowing terms, because I have a lot of respect for her. I can't understand why some people feel threatened by her, but I think its because she is a strong and independent woman unafraid to speak her mind. That is still somewhat of a shocking position for a first lady to take, even in the 1990s.

A reporter in Hollywood once asked me what I thought of Rush Limbaugh.

"The man is a traitor," I replied.

Anyone who is disrespectful and does nothing but criticize the presidency cannot be a patriotic American, and I believe that as much today as I did when I answered the question. Limbaugh's response was a broadside attack on me in his second book, calling me the president's "half-witted half-brother."

Harry and Linda had asked Limbaugh to make a guest appearance on their situation comedy, *Hearts Afire*, which taped on Friday nights at Studio City. The first Friday in December 1993, Limbaugh decided to visit the set to see the production for himself. Jim Moore and three other friends were with Molly and me to watch the taping, and our band playing during the warm-up. I went down on the floor to meet Mr. Limbaugh and asked him for a personal audience. His bodyguards remained while I asked him to lay off the personal attacks. If he had differences with my brother attack the differences—not the man. Somehow, I don't think Rush was listening.

My conflict with him was simple enough. I didn't understand, then or now, how someone can be so negative *all the time*. Sure, there are things wrong with this country. Continuing to harp on the problems and vilifying the personalities and foibles of those you oppose doesn't get us any closer to solving our problems. I would argue that such constant carping only intensifies our problems.

Those who decry our leaders and our institutions should acknowledge their own accountability. Instead of restating problems and casting blame, they might suggest solutions. Until they do, we have every reason to wonder about their motives.

Limbaugh is mean-spirited toward Bill and me, but his theatrics are minor compared to those the supermarket tabloids engage in. At one point I took a trip to New Jersey to check out a product for endorsement. While I was there, I killed an hour or so in a local restaurant. Two weeks later, one of the tabloids claimed I'd beaten up two women while in the restaurant. I've never struck a woman in my life, and I never will. The gist of the story was that my rude behavior had made me unwelcome at the White House, although nothing could have been further from the truth.

⊶ LIFE WITH MOLLY ⊷

After several trips to Dallas during the spring of 1993, I finally persuaded Molly Martin to leave her Texas home and come out west to live with me. Her family, her friends, and her job with a communications firm were all in Texas. She'd grown up in Dallas, and she was Texan through and through. However, she came to California to look things over and liked what she saw. Soon, I flew to Dallas and helped her pack up her car, then we started the three-day drive to California.

Molly and I were wildly attracted to each other from the beginning, although I can't say for certain why that was so. We had dissimilar backgrounds—Molly had been a member of the famous Kilgore Rangerettes, whose collective wholesomeness and discipline would have been alien concepts to a twenty-something Roger Clinton. In Dallas, Molly had been a hostess for one of the city's best restaurants—Del Frisco's—before moving into the corporate world as an executive assistant at Blythe-Nelson in Dallas. Very early in our relationship I was certain Molly was the girl I'd been search-ing for. I'd had my share of whirlwind romances, but there had only been one or two other girlfriends. Molly was beautiful, certainly, but she also was quick to laugh, had a marvelous capacity for love and understanding, and we seemed to agree what life was about. The acid test would be if she could handle living with me.

We left Texas on July 3 and spent the fourth in a little Arizona town, watching a lavish fireworks display. It was Tuesday, the sixth of July, when we finally made it to Los Angeles. I was renting an apartment in Marina del Rey. She took a job working a few hours a day, doing computer entry for a couple of entrepreneuring friends of ours. I was pleased and impressed with Molly's transition to California life. My friends all loved her, of course, and she enjoyed getting to know them. She also helped get me organized, adding a much-needed domestic touch to my apartment.

It wasn't just my apartment that needed a bit of domestic help. I was a hopeless housekeeper. Strangely inspired one day, I decided to polish the hardwood kitchen floor and used a spray can of Pledge for this purpose. By the time I had finished, the floor was nice and shiny but you couldn't get across it without ice skates. It was as slick as a hockey rink.

In the early fall, Molly began to suspect she might be pregnant. Although she'd mentioned it to me, I hadn't taken the thought seriously. Call it denial, but I wasn't overly concerned. Molly went to the store where we did our shopping, Ralph's, and bought a home pregnancy test kit. When the results were positive I scoffed at the method.

"Dr. Ralph told you you're pregnant," I laughed.

Molly went to a clinic in Marina del Rey. They gave her a urine test and again the results were positive. Once again, I didn't believe it.

"There's only one way to settle this," I told her, "and that's to go to a real doctor."

New to southern California, Molly had to find a doctor she felt comfortable with. After finding one, we went to the appointment together. I didn't go into the examining room with her. If she was pregnant, I wanted her to tell me, not the doctor. I waited, anxiously flipping through magazines and watching the other patients walk in and out. Molly returned to the waiting area and stood in front of me.

"I'm pregnant," she said simply. "About eight weeks along."

"Oh, my God," was all I could say. "Oh, my God."

Depend on it, Sir, Samuel Johnson wrote, when a man knows he's to be hanged in a fortnight, it concentrates his mind wonderfully.

I *knew* I wanted to marry Molly, and I *knew* I wanted to spend the rest of my life with her, but somehow I felt this noose tighten around my neck. There are always alternatives when you're faced with a situation like ours, but we didn't consider any of them. I believe—as much as I believe anything—that it's a woman's right to choose what she does with her own body. Regardless, Molly never considered aborting the pregnancy, and I told her I wanted to do whatever she wanted. I knew she wanted to have the baby. She knew I wanted her to have the baby. Today, watching Tyler crawl around on the floor, I know we made the right decision, or rather, that Molly made the right decision.

Molly's pregnancy helped us begin examining our relationship more seriously. Living together was one thing but being married was something else, and I confess I was apprehensive about the entire process. Now, with the baby on the way, we had to put our fears behind us.

Somehow, in the next few months, we became confident enough in our relationship and our love for each other to take the next step. The fall of 1993 was a busy time for us. We were discussing our wedding, planning for a big family Christmas in Washington, and Molly's friends, excited when she told them about the baby, were planning showers and celebrations. We moved into a three-bedroom, two-story condo in North

Redondo Beach, and Jim Moore came out in November and early December to begin working on this book.

My days were busy with rehearsal sessions, interviews, and business meetings. On the weekends, Molly and I would sleep in, then eat brunch somewhere late Saturday morning, and spend the evening together. My Sundays were—and still are—reserved for sporting events on the tube. I'm partial to watching football, but if it's not football season, basketball, baseball, or tennis will do. Of course, I also love to watch televised horse racing.

My recording career was coming to life as well. I'd signed an album deal and began selecting songs for the album. Invitations to perform in far-away places like Korea meant I had to learn to schedule myself. At the request of my record label, I quit my production assistant work, although the band and I still entertained the studio audience on Friday nights.

At Studio City, everyone seemed glad about the success I was enjoying. I even appeared—albeit briefly—in two motion pictures. The year slid past and Molly and I were enjoying our life together. My so-called "celebrity" status was more blessing than burden. By the time Christmas 1993 rolled around, my future looked as bright as the California sunshine. Molly and I packed our clothes, got on a plane, and flew to Washington, D.C., for our first Christmas at the White House.

⇒ FIRST FAMILY CHRISTMAS ⇐

We arrived several days before the holiday to have plenty of time to shop for Christmas presents. Mother was there, too. Trooping into the White House and upstairs to the family quarters, I thought this holiday would be absolutely perfect.

When you get off the elevator on the second floor of the White House, Bill and Hillary's bedroom is on the right. They have a kitchen there as well, which they use often to prepare snacks and drinks. Their bedroom is large, as you might expect, and the kitchen is about the size of a typical suburban kitchen. The other bedrooms are to the left of the elevator.

Mother and Dick were in the Queen's bedroom, where they had slept on Bill's first night in the White House. (It's the room Winston Churchill used when he stayed there; they say Churchill used to scare everyone to death by appearing in the hallway stark naked.) Molly had an ornate bedroom with lovely decor and a high canopied bed. Her room adjoined mine, which looked for all the world like something you'd find at a Holiday Inn. There were two twin beds, and that was it. I decided to grin and make the best of it. For what it's worth, Bill and Hillary did not make the room assignments, the White House staff did.

We ate meals in the solarium on the third floor, which is probably the most beautiful dining area in the nation's capitol. There are windows everywhere, and the view of the Washington Monument and the Capitol is breathtaking at all times of the year. When snow is on the ground, the glare is almost blinding, and in spring the view is of a riot of cherry and dogwood blossoms. At this time of year, we saw festive holiday decorations. Mother, of course, had come to Washington completely prepared for Christmas. Now, I don't know where Bill and I get it, but we have a special holiday tradition of our own and do our shopping at the last minute. This year, though, Molly guided me out of the White House and into the malls a good day and a half before Christmas, even though I really wanted to sit back and watch television with my brother. We headed for Pentagon City, a huge, four-story shopping complex—the biggest mall I've ever been in. The first floor is a food court, and the upper three stories are shops and stores. Bill headed out to shop in Georgetown and Union Station. I guess I thought Molly and I could slip into the crowds of people, buy what we wanted, and return quickly to the White House. But at virtually every stop someone recognized me.

"There's Roger Clinton," I'd hear someone say. Or, "There's the president's brother."

People would walk up to me while I was paying for our gifts. They'd tell me how my brother was doing, what they thought about the country, and many would mention they'd seen me on television. The amazing thing was that about seventy-five percent of the comments I got were positive and upbeat. Most of the people I talked to seemed genuinely glad to meet me, and their warmth added greatly to our Christmas.

Christmas at the White House was wonderful, except for the fact that Bill had to work. As president, he can't just walk out of the oval office at 4:00 P.M. on Christmas Eve afternoon and call it a day. There's always something he needs to look at, someone he needs to talk to. Being in the first family makes for complicated holidays...and complicated departures. Mother and I share a common trait—we enjoy three or four days of vacation, then want to get back home. Bill wanted to fly back to Arkansas with us on Air Force One, and we planned to leave the day after Christmas. Then we discovered that the big 747 can't land on the Hot Springs runway—it's not long enough. We'd fly the smaller 727 instead.

On the morning after Christmas, we were packing to leave when Bill walked out of the elevator. "I can't leave for another day or so," he said, and that was it. We didn't ask why; we knew Bill would not have postponed our return unless something important had come up. Mother and I got on the phone, calling commercial flights. We wanted *out*, and we didn't want to wait another couple of days. As it turned out, we were able to leave late the next day.

In her professional career and in her personal life, Mother was always on time. No matter what the event, she was always punctual. Bill and I did not inherit that trait and tend instead to run on "Clinton Time." That would generally be known elsewhere as late. I often get to airport gates just as they're closing the door of the airplane. When he was governor, Bill would frequently sit back and talk with groups of schoolchildren who came to visit him, unaware that others were cooling their heels in his office. I'm still guilty of running on Clinton time, but Bill has improved since becoming president.

My friends know that I often run late; to a certain extent, they expect it and plan for it. Once, when Jim Moore picked me up at Molly's mother's house in Dallas, he was fifteen minutes late—rare for Jim.

For once, I was ready on time, but Jim wasn't there. "I ought to kick you," I jokingly told him, to which he responded that he was only running on "Roger Clinton Time."

Fair enough.

Mother, Molly, Bill, and I arrived back in Hot Springs late on December 27. We spent three days at home, then Bill returned to the White House. Molly and I went to Dallas. Mother flew to Las Vegas. Later Molly and I joined her there for New Year's Eve. Barbra Streisand was performing at the new MGM Grand. We attended one of her two shows, and spent the rest of our time in the casino. There, in the Sportsbook, we watched the ponies run. It was on videotape, but the wagering was real enough. We were given racing forms which we studied just as if we were watching the horses at Oaklawn racetrack. Then we'd place our bets, watch the video, count the money, and get ready for the next race.

When we had a chance, we would sit side-by-side at the quarter slot machines, dropping in coins, watching the reels spin, and sharing each other's excitement if one of us hit the jackpot. I haven't spent much time in Las Vegas, but it isn't because I don't have fun there.

Mother's health had continued to deteriorate during the past few months, and she spent most of her time in Las Vegas in a wheelchair. Still, she seemed to have plenty of energy, and she was obviously having the time of her life. I'll never forget how vibrant and alive she was.

As holidays go, Christmas and New Year's 1993 will be times I'll remember for the rest of my life. When they were over, however, I felt I needed to get back home to work. Mother and I said our good-byes in Las Vegas, and I took a commuter flight to Los Angeles. Molly and I spent the next couple of days recovering from the long holiday. Bear, our dog, was glad we were home, and so were we.

DADO'S PASSING

The telephone rang about 11:30 at night.

I was still up, watching television in the living room. My answering machine played its message, then I listened to the White House operator ask if I could speak to the president. I picked up the phone and waited the few seconds for the connection.

"Roger," Bill's voice intoned, "Mother just died."

The world seemed to spin out of control as I dropped to the floor. Mother had held us together as a family, given Bill the strength to carry despite his tumultuous first year as president, and guided me through my own changing life.

"Try to get hold of yourself," Bill told me, but I couldn't.

He kept trying to console me, but I was in the depths of despair and anguish. Finally, Bill seemed to understand I had to deal with this in my own way—even if my own way was hysteria.

"I'll call you back when I know more," he said, and hung up.

Molly came into the living room and sat down beside me. She took the phone out of my hand, then hugged me and held me as if I were a child. I was screaming and crying and it took several minutes before I could settle down enough to call Dick Kelley.

Dick told me Mother had died in her sleep. She had gone to bed as usual around 8:00 P.M. and when Dick went to check on her around 1:00 A.M. she was gone. She had died without suffering.

Molly continued to hold me, but grief descended upon me, cold and sharp. In time, I calmed down enough to think ahead, and since I couldn't sleep, I began making arrangements to go back to Arkansas.

Bill called back to tell me that he would fly home late that day. It was just after 3:00 A.M., January 6, in Washington—past midnight in California.

On the morning of January 7, Bill and I went to the funeral home to say a private good-bye to Mother. I put cassettes of some of the songs from my album and a photo of Mother and me together into her casket. I wanted her to sleep with my music beside her.

There wasn't a church in Hot Springs big enough for her funeral. I know that Reverend John Miles, Mother's friend for years, had considered holding the service at Oaklawn racetrack, but we ended up having it in the Civic Center.

Three thousand people attended the service. Mother was mourned by United States senators, governors, entertainers, and athletes. Barbra Streisand was there, too. She and Mother had developed a special relationship based on admiration, respect, and a true love for each other. Mother would have been pleased with the funeral.

"Virginia," Brother John said, "was an American original."

Bill and I followed the hearse eighty miles to Hope, where Mother would be laid to rest in Rose Hill cemetery next to my grandparents and Bill's father, Bill Blythe. People pulled over to the side of the road and watched us pass. Some had small American flags in their hands. Others held their hands over their hearts. During the service at the cemetery, Brother John told the crowd that Mother "was like a rubber ball. The harder life put her down, the higher she bounced. She didn't know what the word 'quit' meant."

After the service, before they closed Mother's casket for the final time, I laid more gifts beside her. At Christmas, Molly and I had given her a small book about grandmothers. Before the funeral, I inscribed the book as if the message were being written by my as-yet-unborn child: "Dear Ginger, I've heard a lot of good things about you already. I can't wait to meet you." It was Tyler's gift to Mother. I signed the book "Cassidy" because at the time Molly and I didn't know whether we'd have a boy or girl. If we had a girl, we intended to name her Cassidy D'Ann. A boy would be named Tyler Cassidy. Cassidy is my middle name, and it was Mother's maiden name. D'Ann is Molly's middle name. I slipped the book beside Mother's hands, and Bill and I watched as the coffin was lowered into the ground.

Almost immediately following the funeral, Bill left for an overseas conference. Hillary and Chelsea went back to the White

House. I felt bereft, but Molly helped me through the next several days until we flew back to California on Monday, January 10. We'd been home for a week when the earthquake hit on January 17, 1994.

About 3:30 that morning, Bear, our dog, started barking, waking us as he bounded into the bedroom and roamed around acting as if someone was in the house. His ears were tucked back and he was obviously scared. We had no idea what he was looking for, but we finally got him calmed down enough to get back to sleep.

A few minutes later the earthquake hit, shaking the house. Molly screamed.

"I love you," I told her as the shock waves slammed us up and down. "We just have to ride it out. There's nothing we can do."

The tremors were shaking the house so violently, I thought the walls would collapse at any moment. In my mind's eye, I pictured Molly and myself pinned beneath piles of rubble. The three of us huddled in bed together, Molly and I crying and Bear whimpering loudly.

Four or five minutes later, the pounding ceased as suddenly as it had begun. There would be the inevitable aftershocks, but the worst of the quake was apparently over. The power was out, and we had to wait a few hours until dawn to survey the damage.

As word of the disaster spread across the country, the telephone started to ring. Bill called from the White House. We told him we were okay and hung up quickly, anxious to avoid jamming the phone lines. As it grew light outside, we discovered a couple of good-sized cracks in the plaster walls although it appeared that the frame of the house had absorbed most of the shock. A few kitchen dishes had bounced out of the cabinets and lay smashed and broken on the floor. Some of our wall hangings had fallen and the rest hung lopsided. We were more fortunate than many in our area and very thankful for it.

We were barely seventeen days into the New Year and already Mother had died and we'd lived through a major earthquake. Molly and I began to consider other events that might befall us, and we were worried about our wedding. While we were planning our Christmas trip to Washington, Bill and Hillary had offered to let us get married at the White House. In retrospect, I can see that Bill had forecast Mother's decline and wanted to make sure she would be alive to see me get married. However, Molly and I did not want a White House wedding for fear that the event would turn into a media circus. Neither of us wanted our family and friends subjected to the scrutiny of the press.

Instead, we set the date for March 26 in the Dallas Arboretum, a relatively small facility. The media wouldn't be intrusive there, we felt sure. The guest list, as I saw it, was largely for Mother, or rather, for her memory. The event itself was designed to entertain our friends. I was marrying Molly for myself and for her. But when we put together the guest list and the invitations, I tried to invite the people Mother would have. I invited her birthday club, a group of twelve women, including Mother's best friends in Hot Springs, who met for lunch once a month. I also invited the members of the "Clinton Connection," those folks in Arkansas who had worked for Bill in every election since his first campaign for Congress.

I think we sent out over seven hundred invitations and about five hundred fifty people attended. The seating area was full an hour before the ceremony. Many of those who got to the Arboretum in plenty of time had to stand up throughout the entire ceremony and reception. The size of the crowd didn't help my nerves. In our dressing room at the Arboretum, Bill tried to help me relax.

"This is just like jumping out of an airplane—without a parachute," he said.

I was glad I didn't know what he meant. He put his arms around me and told me how proud Mother would be to see me on this day.

"She's here," Bill told me.

⟞⟝ GOING TO THE CHAPEL ⟞⟝

The preparations for the wedding had gone smoothly enough. Molly's mother, Emilie, had done a wonderful job. Now, we were minutes away from the start of the ceremony. I was anxious, short of breath, and felt an incredible need to cry.

"It's going to be okay," Bill told me, shaking me gently by the shoulders of my tuxedo.

Bill was my best man. He and the groomsmen were dressed as I was, in black. My eyes kept welling with tears; I was over-whelmed and also missed Mother.

I pulled myself together and resolved to walk down the aisle knowing I was the happiest and luckiest guy on the planet. Then Brother John walked in.

"Roger," he said, "it's time."

"Time, Brother John? Already?"

Bill put his arm around me.

"It's going to be okay," he told me again, and gently pushed me toward the door.

Outside, the crowd of hundreds was waiting to watch us walk down the aisle. Brother John led the procession as Bill, my groomsmen, and I made our way to the altar. We stood there, waiting for Molly, and I couldn't keep my hands from shaking. Soon enough, spasms of anxiety engulfed my entire body. A few people in the crowd laughed. I clasped my hands to keep them from shaking, and leaned my head on Brother John's shoulder for support.

We watched Molly walk down the aisle, her sisters and friends preceeding her as bridesmaids. She looked angelic in her white dress and her walk toward the altar certainly seemed an eternity. When she finally stood beside me, we turned to face Brother John, who had a little speech all ready, much to my surprise. He told me—with the crowd listening, of course—that he wanted to talk to me a minute before I got married. Some of the members of the audience chuckled. In the next sentence, he mentioned Mother's name. Instantly, a loud clap of thunder sounded overhead, and I nearly jumped out of my tux. I was certain Mother was out there, and the thunder was her way of letting us know she was watching.

Brother John talked to me for a moment about the kind of responsibility I was accepting. His chat lasted perhaps a minute— it was very fatherly. He finished, and Molly and I recited our vows. I had just lifted her veil and kissed the bride when the skies opened up and a deluge poured down upon us. Within minutes, the awning covering the guests and the wedding party sagged under the weight of the water. Lightning danced across White Rock Lake. The Arboretum grass, the flowers, the band—all were washed clean.

Molly and I dashed for the sanctuary of the Arboretum's main building, where our reception was to begin. The guests filed in as quickly as they could, and enjoyed refreshments while Bill and Hillary, Molly and I, her mother, and the wedding party posed for photographs. We came downstairs to cut the cake. My big brother helped serve the guests cake.

Bill, Hillary, and Chelsea left after a couple of hours at the reception. Even though the Secret Service had checked all our guests, running everyone through a metal detector, they seemed anxious to get Bill out of there. Molly and I stayed another hour, then we also left.

If I sound a little vague talking about the reception, there's a good reason why. I don't remember much of it. It remains a blur to me, and I can't remember who I greeted or who I held long conversations with. I understand that loss of memory is a natural consequence of getting married, but I didn't think it would affect me so soon.

Molly and I went back to the Mansion on Turtle Creek, a posh Dallas hotel where Bill and Hillary were staying. I'd stayed there for the day before the wedding, and Molly and I spent our wedding night there. The next day, a Sunday, we went downtown to Reunion Arena, where Bill and I watched the Arkansas Razorbacks in the NCAA basketball tournament finals. Molly was beside me; she may have been bored by the game, but she seemed happy to be there.

We returned to California a few days later. At the time of the wedding, she was seven months' pregnant and we didn't think it wise to plan a honeymoon because of her condition. Our thought was to wait for the baby, and then plan a trip for the three of us. Perhaps you know how it is with a new baby. Tyler is nine months old as of this writing and we still haven't gone on that trip.

Following the wedding, I devoted most of my time to the final details of my upcoming album. I had been to Lookout Mountain, Georgia, twice in late 1993 to record ten cuts, and I now had the chance to hear the post-production versions. I was excited by what I heard, naturally, but I had yet to see the completely finished product. As with many products, the packaging for a compact disc is probably more important to sales than what's inside.

The jewel box (jargon for CD box) liner notes were ready late in the summer of 1994, and I was extremely pleased with the outstanding job the photographer, Jeff Katz, and the designer, Hugh Syme, had done. Vicki Crawford and I had helped with the concept. The cover shot shows me in front of a small frame house that's brilliantly lit from the inside. I'm standing next to a sidewalk, an Arkansas boulder at my feet, and the house is ringed by greenery.

Two white lawn chairs on the porch give the house a lived-in look and the entire scene is very warm and down-home. To my right and behind me is a bright yellow convertible that reminds me of the Henry J. that Bill and I drove around in when I was little. When you take the liner notes out of the compact disc jewel box and unfold them, the picture takes on a whole new dimension. The house, the car, and I are standing high atop a desert butte. The liner notes were a perfect visualization for the title of the album, "Nothing Good Comes Easy." The title track, which A. G. Sun, "Bear" Schuchner, and I wrote, is a tribute to Mother and her philosophy of life. It's my favorite song on the album.

"Nothing Good Comes Easy" doesn't top the list for anyone except me. "Fantasy of Love" was released to national airplay and as a cassette single some weeks before the album came out in September. This song has a strong coastal feel to it; it's a smooth, Carribbean love song. "Ain't No Cure for You" is almost a country crossover song, a lament about lost love.

The release of the album in September was a very fulfilling and satisfying experience. It felt like a part of me was being sold on music store shelves. Of course, any artist feels that way when something he or she has created becomes available to the public. I hope to experience it again and again.

We began planning the promotional efforts for the compact disc early in 1994. In addition to giving several hundred live radio interviews, I'd be performing in key markets around the country. Complicating the schedule was the fact that I'd been invited to perform in Korea during the first week in October. The Korean trip was for a good cause—a joint American and Korean benefit for the handicapped children of Korea. As it happened, I didn't make the trip until late January of 1995 because the incident involving the downed United States helicopter forced another delay. I finally went to Korea, did the show, and was gratified to have helped raise a great deal of money for such a worthy cause.

Foreign audiences are drawn to my "First Brother" status, perhaps as much or more than they are to the music. Many people outside this country see me as the closest they'll ever come to meeting Bill Clinton, and I guess I'm a bit of a curiousity. Nonetheless, I've had outstanding responses from audiences in Germany, Argentina, and Spain. Wherever I've gone—for an interview or to perform with my band—the crowds have been overwhelmingly positive and supportive.

⇒ A NEW BABY CLINTON ⇐

Tyler Cassidy Clinton made his first appearance to a packed hospital delivery room on May 12, 1994. Molly's labor had to be induced and we had the option to wait a couple of days—for Friday the 13th to pass—or have the baby on the twelfth.

"I'm not carrying this kid around for two more days," Molly told the doctors.

We flew Molly's mother, Emilie, out to California on May 11. I know Emilie's presence really helped Molly, and she was a comfort to me, too. After all, I was about to become a father. There were still so many things to learn, and Emilie is a pro when it comes to kids. Before Molly and I were married, Emilie told me she knew she couldn't take the place of Mother but she said she wanted to be as much of a mother to me as she could. Just then, with Molly's labor about to begin, I was awfully glad Emilie was there beside me.

We rolled into the parking lot of the Little Company of Mary Hospital in North Redondo Beach just after 8:00 A.M. on May 12. Tyler Cassidy was born at 2:07 P.M., weighing in at eight pounds, two ounces. I stood beside Molly and held her hand, and the doctors allowed Emilie to come into the delivery room.

A good friend of ours stood at Molly's head and shot video of the birth. Believe it or not, I didn't freak out in the delivery room, even though Molly and all our friends were betting I would. The toughest moment occurred when the doctor handed Tyler to me. Fortunately, I didn't drop him or anything, but I was a mess emotionally. Throughout the labor, I had held Molly's hand and coached her breathing and now I had my son in my arms. I think it fair to say I was visably more excited at Tyler's birth than either Emilie or Molly—Molly was half asleep. I was the most excited new father *ever*. Emilie has ten other grandchildren so the process wasn't new to her, although watching a delivery was.

"Overwhelmed and excited," she describes me at Tyler's birth.

Who wouldn't be? We had our portable phone in the delivery room, and I dialed the White House switchboard. I told them the situation, and they put me through to Bill.

"Here's Tyler," I told Bill, "and he has something to say to you."

I held out the phone to pick up the sounds of Tyler's crying. Molly wasn't sure who was crying more loudly, Tyler or me. I suspect that, by the time we hung up, Bill was crying, too. We took Molly and Tyler back home a day later. I was a little stiff with him at first, requiring some coaching from Emilie, but I soon managed to hold Tyler, burp him after Molly had finished nursing, and change his diaper without mishap. Emilie was quite proud, and I only wished Mother could have been there as well.

Emilie flew home to Texas a few days later, certain she had left her new grandson in good hands. It was nearly a month before Tyler met his uncle, the president. Bill came to Los Angeles, and we took Tyler to the Sheraton Santa Monica to meet him. From the smile on his face, it was evident he was delighted to see his new nephew. Bill, I could tell, was very proud of Molly and me, and I'm sure it's clear that we were rather proud of ourselves. Tyler was the most important thing in our lives. Regardless of what else Molly and I did, Tyler would always be our greatest accomplishment.

Bill treated Tyler almost reverently. "Hi, Tyler," he said as he picked up Tyler and held him close, "I'm your Uncle Bill."

Uncle Bill played some of the silly games parents play with babies. This was a different side of Bill I had not been around to see when Chelsea was a baby. Then he talked to Tyler as if the baby were an adult, capable of understanding every word. The baby seemed to return his respect and affection. We took several photos of Bill holding Tyler, both of them actually looking at the camera lens.

Bill bounced Tyler around a bit, then he sat down on the sofa with the baby on his lap and reached for the telephone. It took a few minutes to put the call through to Hillary. Even though Bill had the handset to his ear, Molly and I heard Hillary pick up the telephone.

"Hey," Bill said, "I'm sitting here with my nephew in my lap."

In the next breath, Bill was telling Hillary what a beautiful baby Tyler was. I was too proud for words. I was married to a beautiful woman, my life was back on track, and my brother was president of the United States. Our baby was sitting in his lap. Tyler was the next generation, ready to explore the joys and sorrows of growing up Clinton.

My eyes filled up with tears. I turned away from Bill, and looked out the window toward the ocean. When I'm feeling really good, I always start to cry.